"Jason Shulman brilliantly integrates a deep psychological component with a profound understanding of the non-dual, absolute unity of the Divine Nature in a way that raises the reader's soul to the highest potential of awareness. While traditional teachings tend to demean the ego-self, Shulman shows us the importance of our gift of self-awareness and how to come to peace with ourselves. Thus he leads readers to evoke a healing from our sense of fractured separation into a wholeness of being that has compassion for who we are and what we are. This is a must-read for anyone who wishes to learn the essence of kabbalistic teachings in the hands of a master of spiritual and psychological development."

RABBI DAVID A. COOPER, author of *God Is a Verb*

"Here is once and future wisdom as we meet the Jewish mystical tradition in its revelatory mapping of the nature of reality. Here too are practices that bring the reader closer to the nondual state of consciousness and awareness of the integral relationship between all things. Taken seriously, this profound work can only charge the spirit as it illumines the mind and heart."

JEAN HOUSTON, PH.D., author of *Jump Time: Shaping Your Future in a World of Radical Change*

"Jason Shulman is a true adept of the inner teachings. He offers a very sophisticated and dynamic account of what happens between the Kabbalah and the great, luminous transparency. To engage with Jason Shulman's mind is to enter into the reality where true healing can occur."

RABBI ZALMAN SCHACHTER-SHALOMI,
leader of the Jewish Renewal Movement
and coauthor of *From Age-ing to Sage-ing*

"*Kabbalistic Healing* is a great book about discovering wisdom within each of us. At a time when everyone in contemporary society is experiencing an information glut, what's missing is a deeper understanding of life. Jason Shulman provides the reader with wisdom and insight for life's journey."

STEPHAN RECHTSCHAFFEN, cofounder and CEO of the Omega Institute for Holistic Studies

"Jason Shulman is a sincere, authentic practitioner of Kabbalah. The fruit of much inner work, the masterful teachings in this book resonate and come alive because he has truly experienced this wisdom from deep inside."

RABBI TIRZAH FIRESTONE, author of *The Receiving: Reclaiming Jewish Women's Wisdom* and *With Roots in Heaven*

"We can whole-heartedly embrace these pristine teachings of Jason Shulman, in particular Jason's Massachusetts bagel shop experience, which conveys the true essence of Zen. Thank you, Jason, for your hard work. We all benefit. May we all live and be well."

SHAKA KENDO RICH HART, Abbot of Clear Mountain Zen Center

"Jason Shulman is a living Kabbalist, a master who transcends the narrowness of academic Kabbalah and the superficiality of popular Kabbalah. He lives and breathes new life into the ancient tradition through the profound intuitions of his own awakened soul. This is one of those rare books that inspires you to live higher, deeper and better than you ever thought was possible. Accept Reb Jason's invitation to your soul's adventure, and you will have taken a critical step on your own path to healing and transformation."

RABBI MORDECHAI (MARC) GAFNI, spiritual director of Bayit Chadash Community/Retreat Center, Israel, and author of *Soul Prints*

Kabbalistic Healing

A Path to an Awakened Soul

Jason Shulman

Inner Traditions
Rochester, Vermont

Inner Traditions
One Park Street
Rochester, Vermont 05767
www.InnerTraditions.com

Library of Congress Cataloging-in-Publication Data
Shulman, Jason.
  Kabbalistic healing : a path to an awakened soul / Jason Shulman.
    p. cm.
  ISBN 1-59477-015-8 (pbk.)
  1. Cabala—History. 2. Spiritual life—Judaism. 3. Healing—Religious aspects—Judaism. 4. Spiritual healing. I. Title.
  BM526.S557 2004
  296.7'12—dc22

                                                                        2004013635

Printed and bound in the United States at Capital City Press

10 9 8 7 6 5 4 3 2

Text design and layout by Priscilla Baker
This book was typeset in Sabon

The cover and chapter opening symbol was created by Moses Cordovero circa 1592. It shows the names of the ten sephirot, starting with Keter on the outermost edge to Malchut at the very center of the symbol. It is the symbol of the school founded by Jason Shulman, A Society of Souls.

Contents

ACKNOWLEDGMENTS   vii

INTRODUCTION   1

1 LEAVING THE LIMITED   9

2 LIVING BETWEEN THE LIGHT AND DARK:
THE HOLY EGO   35

3 HEALING, BRIAH, AND THE CONCEPT OF NOT-MAKING   48

4 THE HEALING OF IMMANENCE AND THE NATURE OF GOD   73

5 WITHIN DEATH   95

6 PRAYER: THE CONCRETE PATH   119

7 THE WORDS OF GOD   144

AFTERWORD: IT STARTS WITH A DISAPPOINTMENT . . .

    . . . AND IT ENDS IN LIGHT   168

ABOUT A SOCIETY OF SOULS   174

GLOSSARY   178

To Arlene

❧❀❧

Acknowledgments

I have been incredibly lucky in life. God has always given me the answers that my soul craved, even when I hardly knew the questions. I have many people to thank for healing me, supporting me, and correcting my faults so that I could become who I always was in my heart: a lover of the world's mystery. I would like to single out several people without whose kindness-in-action this book would never have been written.

Norman Trager, master psychotherapist and kindhearted educator, for supporting my life and work in the best possible way: by skill and by example. Rabbi Zalman Schachter-Shalomi, whose tenderness toward me from our very first meeting touched me deeply. He is the man I go to in order to watch him tie his shoes and learn how to approach the big questions.

Finally, with deepest love and respect, I bow to Shaka Kendo Rick Hart, abbot of Clear Mountain Zen Center, my spiritual father, who made me walk on ice so that I could eventually melt my heart. It is through him that I have met the Buddha face-to-face.

I gratefully acknowledge my early spiritual teachers: Alice Coleman, who awakened my love of poetry and taught me to trust the true word, and Eva Pierrakos for her groundbreaking teachings. I also need to thank my students in A Society of Souls for drawing these teachings from me and giving me people with whom to share them.

My deepest gratitude goes to my wife, Arlene, and my daughter, Ariana: Arlene for being my constant teacher and showing me what true love and brilliance are; and Ariana for her emotional genius, her humor, and her fresh fondness for life. Many thanks are also due to Ann Massion, M.D., whose belief in this work was integral in getting this book to the public. My editors, Nancy Yeilding and Jeanie Levitan, also deserve thanks for their skill and the tenderness with which they approached their tasks.

Finally, I bow humbly before the disincarnate teachers who have given me this work in trust, asking me to grow into a man who can speak simply in the world.

Introduction

To study Kabbalah is not to study a subject but to meet a teacher. This is the teacher God sends out to all created things. It is God's kindness and mercy that says, "The world of matter is the place where I am most hidden. This is because to be in matter and to be with Me is no easy thing. It is like breathing out and in at the same time. So I send this living force to you. It is the universal solvent that finds its way through every material that stands in its way. It appears when you call for it. It forms a river that must and always will flow to Me. Enter this stream. To study Kabbalah is to study yourself."

THE KABBALAH—which is the Jewish mystical path of cleaving to God and knowing Reality—speaks to the central fire in our being.

Kabbalah is above all a means of joining with the Divine. It is a path of profound transformation, the fruit of which is to awaken into Life in such a way that our former lives seem like sleep in comparison. It brings about the ultimate healing of the human soul.

From my perspective, the reasons to study Kabbalah are completely practical and human: it lessens the distance between ourselves and others; it lets us see the origins of what truly nourishes us; it reawakens in us the trembling of awe and sex; it brings us to God while we are in the body and makes us men and women truly made in the image of the Intimate One. We study Kabbalah to learn to love

Life and to honor its every piece and see its presence in every way.

While some people take the word *kabbalah,* which can be translated as "received," to be a tradition of already existent metaphysical work that the student learns, Kabbalah for me is the living experience of the Real Self, the self that is always connected to God, the self that lives in God the way a fish lives in water: water inside and water outside.

From the perspective of our yearning for God, Kabbalah is not an advanced study; it is the first study. Kabbalah speaks directly to our fundamental desire to know what life is about, and it emerges naturally, therefore, from the very marrow of our being.

While Kabbalah does include materials received from past teachers—such as Rabbi Isaac the Blind; Isaac Luria, called the Ari; Rabbi Hammai; Moses de Leon; and innumerable, unnamed co-conspirators in the search for God—Kabbalah also means being willing to receive life as the great teaching itself, to see life as God's greatest lesson and God's greatest gift. It means being willing to understand that both of these—the lesson and the gift—always come together and must be received at the same time in order to create illumination.

Because the human ego is what it is, any path, any material that describes the unified state, which is an expression of the living God, can become petrified. So no path can be transmitted secondhand, by words alone, but must be resurrected anew in each person's life. We must do something to quicken the seed that is already within us.

We spend all our lives dying in one way or another. We leave our childhood and our parents. We leave grade school. We enter into adulthood. People leave us, and we begin to see that one day we will leave those who go on without us. If we have been lucky enough to have studied the Kabbalah of life, we will be ready for the moment that we burst from the mountainside of stone into the arms of God.

Once we know this, even if we still have a whole lifetime to live, we are free to worship in every way, each thing, always. We are free because we do not cling to life, as opposed to death. Coming and going are the same for us when we are in God. We see them as one within us, and thereby can see the Real Face of the One who made us.

We serve the divine spirit of Life by finding a way to be true to ourselves. This is true self-realization or God-cleaving. The problem arises when we don't know who we are. So we try to be true to many different versions of ourselves and head out into the wilderness in many different ways, with many different aims and methods.

Ultimately, because we and what we call God are never separate, every path we walk moves us closer to the Real. It is the Real—already within us—that makes this possible. So though we start out differently and with different approaches and aims, we must walk the same territory and arrive at the same place.

This book is about that eternal, verifiable, and dependable process, as examined through my understanding of Kabbalah, the received and continually receivable wisdom of the path of Torah (the foundational text of Judaism and the written law). Judaism is usually thought of as a path that conceives of God as a separate being, but this is not accurate. Beneath the appearance of contemporary Judaism are the tracks of those who have seen God in a nondual way. The written Torah along with the Oral Torah—that portion of the Torah transmitted to and handed down by Moses and interpreted by generations of thinkers—combine to reveal what the Torah truly is: a description of the interaction between Oneness and Duality; a vehicle for finding and cleaving to this Unity, often called God; and a profound explanation of the reasons and direction of Creation.

My kabbalistic work, as I see it, is to seek neither the dualistic God nor the nondual God. In the spirit of kabbalistic exploration—which sees "as above, so below"—my work is to find in each separate thing the Wholeness that is the breath of our Creator. It makes all the difference in the world to know that the One we seek seeks us with greater fervor than we can imagine. Because of that, our seeking must include a form of spiritual relaxation, a kind of staying put while being completely awake, so that God has no trouble finding us. Thus our calling out is caught by God, and returned to us not as an echo of our own small voice, but as something fresh and alive. God simply, above all things, wants us to know the truth.

If we could pronounce the unpronounceable Name of God, what would the light of this Name illuminate? It would bring out the spark in the eyes of the Jews of Safed, past, present, and future. It would shine in the eyes of Arabs in Brooklyn worshipping Allah, and of Native Americans chanting to the grandfather and grandmother Spirits; it would sanctify the Christians' love of the one who showed them how to be one with the Father. It would illuminate each group loving God in its own way.

Apparent contradictions on the surface of things often show us that a deeper unity lies beneath. For example, what some people call God or the Real Self, Awakening or Submission, Buddha-nature or the Real, are all the same thing: the language life uses to talk about Life. So while this book may use one or another word or name to describe this intrinsic holiness, please use them all in a way that makes your own journey possible.

Kabbalistic Healing is about both the process of unification and the implications of that process for daily life. Above all, this book is meant to be directly transformative itself. It is meant not only to be information that, once taken in by the mind, can be used or filed away, but an agent of change, a way of translating ourselves from our trance state of separateness to the state of being with God.

The tradition of this type of "teaching text" is long and established in kabbalistic literature. The deepest meanings of these texts are closed to careless or casual perusal; their words reveal themselves fully only to the reader who works with each concept and goes through a transformative process that actually changes the level of his or her comprehension.

Like these ancient texts, *Kabbalistic Healing* offers the possibility of knowing God directly. Unlike other modern works on the Kabbalah, this book is not a rehash of older ideas. Instead, it is a journey through kabbalistic concepts, connections, and relationships from the perspective of joining with Reality, the perspective that is at the heart of Kabbalah.

All journeys begin with a question. In this case, it is our soul that speaks:

"Why study Kabbalah?"

"To know God."

"Why must we know God?"

"Because God is not separate from us in any way. God is our inner-most tissue, our closer-than-closest self, and we have a desire to know ourselves, to understand the world around us—which is also God—and so we search for what we know is there."

"Isn't it enough to follow our religions as they were handed down to us?"

"Perhaps. But because they were handed down to us, we run the risk of only getting to know God secondhand, someone else's God. God cannot be known secondhand. Sooner or later, if you are in touch with the inner drive to understand, through bodily excitement or through the pain of life, you want to know directly, and that is when the metaphysical approach to knowing comes into play. Kabbalah is simply the understanding and encouragement handed down through the centuries from people who have done what you want to do. They stand there, their immortal parts still calling, still present, saying, 'Here is how you can learn for yourself. Here is the courage to try.'"

Within each human being is both a universe held in common with all other beings and a unique universe that is that individual's portion of Heaven, for that person alone to reveal. I hope this book encourages each of us to shine with our own portion of Heaven and teaches us simultaneously how to be illuminated by the light of others. We need not be afraid of each other or afraid of differences. But as God made the choices of Creation, separating day from night, we need not fear choosing our own way, touched to the blood by what flows within us.

This life may be a mystery, but it is a mystery of Love. We simply need to know how to surrender to what God gives us, like manna, each day. We are a species of beings who cannot afford to leave the gifts of Heaven lying on the ground any longer, but must lift them up, bring them to the table, and eat.

It is to the continuing spirit of basic sanity in all people that I offer this book. My hope is that we may awaken from our self-imposed slumber and find that within the myriad appearances of the world lies the single fact of the truth of God, of the many becoming one again, of the One in every created thing.

This book represents my own understanding of the nature of God, Reality, and its illumination through Kabbalah. It is the work I have been doing for over thirty years. I carry on my work through A Society of Souls, a school dedicated to the awakening of the human spirit through the work of Integrated Kabbalistic Healing, IM/personal Movement, and the Work of Return. It is in this forum that I have the privilege of teaching students who are passionately interested in the same thing that brought me to this study: human liberation from the small view and a passionate desire to know the truth of God.

In some of the chapters you will find brief questions posed by either students in A Society of Souls or people at public talks I have given around the country. These questions have always allowed me to go deeper into the work and for that I am grateful. For those of you interested in finding out more about the work offered by ASOS, further information is included at the end of this book.

As a kabbalistic text, *Kabbalistic Healing* may be studied on different levels. The casual reader, interested in finding out more about the kabbalistic perspective, will find stimulating ideas that are provocative and instructive. But for those who want more, this book can serve as a vehicle that can carry you to a new level of integration and understanding. The following suggestions may help you ride the words in this book to your Real Self, the Self that is always with God.

Relax. Kabbalistic works are not about grasping. It is our ego that grasps, trying to hold the entire world in its small hands. In order to learn something new, we must let go of the tired and true. When some ideas are not immediately clear, let them pass and return to them later. The sun often shines after a cloudy day.

Persevere. Traditional texts were always read many times. While the ego would like to have everything revealed upon demand, we must be willing to bear some frustration. My advice is to read everything over again. When you come to a passage that seems difficult, remember that reading Kabbalah is more like an encounter with a living being, like meeting a person for the first time.

Let it take you where your soul wants to go. There will be many moments while reading this book when you need to pause to fully consider what is being said. These moments of stillness are often the most productive moments. Kabbalistic learning asks us to turn to these moments of silent contemplation to transform our limited concepts of ourselves. The pauses bring us to a new level of understanding, one that can be reached only by wholehearted waiting instead of always pressing forward.

Question everything! Nothing is out of bounds. Let the words of this book challenge you, and let yourself challenge the book as well. In this way, you will have a dialogue with the words of this text, and in the time-honored way of Kabbalah, the truth will emerge.

Read portions aloud. This book, though in printed form, really harkens back to the oral tradition of teaching and transmission. By reading passages aloud, you will be taught not only by the ideas, but also by the rhythms and sounds of the words themselves.

Remember that you have friends in high places. Sometimes, if we do not get an immediate answer to our inquiry, we feel abandoned. My advice is to breathe and follow the first suggestion: *Relax.* Know that if you ask with your heart, your heart will be answered. We are all answered in the language in which we ask our questions. It is also true that the universe supports our inquiry into Reality in many invisible ways, and we will all receive unending support whenever we ask.

Entering the book, you will find chapters that deal with prayer; with the concept of nonduality and God; with death, the ego, psychotherapy, and other topics. It is important to me to state from the onset that all of these chapters, which include the details of human life and the particulars of Kabbalah, are really about the human heart and its place in the vast universe. They are meant to open the mind and heart to a new way of walking our seasons on Earth so that whatever the weather, our years are filled with harvest.

Above all, I have tried to construct a book of love. Some of it is philosophical love; some of it is thought-filled love; some of it is funny, some of it sad, some of it mysterious, some of it enlightening. I have tried to fashion into words the love I feel for all of creation. This book is primarily a transmission. My wish is that it be a useful tool in making it easier for people to change into who they truly are: creatures of Light with the vast potential of Love.

Finally, I urge readers to use their own wisdom. Spiritual learning in whatever tradition always comes down to two complementary streams: we need to make the effort to quest and find and we also need to know that there is nothing to search for, that we have been Whole from the beginning.

ONE

Leaving the Limited

The Kabbalah is a wonderful tool for looking at how we make the world over in our own image. It is a wonderful tool because the Kabbalah is not a series of books or a series of theories, but a course in experience. It actually asks us to participate in the world in a new way. It asks us to be awake, to engage, and to awaken to that engagement. When we are awake to such participation, something entirely different reveals itself. This revelation would not occur if we still believed that we were working on an objective theory about the world rather than participating in the making of that world.

KABBALAH IS A PARADIGM that asks us to step out of the static, snapshot quality of our usual mode of thinking, and to enter what the physicist David Bohm has called the *implicate order,* the enfolded order. This enfolded order is difficult to talk about and difficult to conceptualize, since it is not born of words but of experience. All of us have experienced it many times in our lifetime: those moments that all things seemed to somehow make sense to us; where life and all its myriad difficulties were somehow all right; when the face of some silent perfection—that even includes imperfection—peered through our discursive mind. The problem for us humans, however, is how to both name this state—since naming gives it a home in our bodymind—and continue in it, despite and along with the difficulties of being human. This is our path: to continue to participate in the way things are.

When we begin experiencing this participatory reality, we could say that we are in the awakened state, which in theistic language we might call "being in the presence of God." The awakened state is realizing that there is a third thing going on between us and the world that is neither "us" nor "the world." It is the realization that there is total relationship going on all of the time that completely changes the context of our lives. This awakened or *relational* state happens when we leave the still picture for a living relationship with the All, which I think of as what the Buddhists call Clear Light and the kabbalists describe as the Light of Paradise. This light is the Light of the world.

The deeper we go into the world, the more we find God at the center of everything. Because God is at the center of everything, we might ask ourselves why we need to study the world so carefully. The reason is this: so that we can know creation. While the essential truth is easy— God is everything and God is everywhere—knowing how this truth plays itself out in the world of duality is of utmost importance. We need to know how to act. We need to know how to be so that we can reduce the enormous suffering in the world. The best way to do that is from the position of understanding the Divine core around which the world is built—indeed, *of which* the world is built.

Over the years, my studies and teaching have brought me to the understanding that God and the world are truly One, and that only a nondual perspective will help us to open our hearts to ourselves and others. If we can understand any part of the human story freshly, which means we understand it with more depth, and if our understanding is a truthful version of things, it will lead to more compassion in the way we work with other people and the way we work with ourselves. If we revisit even fundamental aspects of our personal psychology using the fresh approach that comes from a nondual perspective, we open the door to seeing ourselves in a new way, thereby opening new possibilities for healing ourselves and the world.

THE UNCONSCIOUS REVEALED

I would like to suggest a possible route for us to think in a new way about the unconscious. But to approach this new understanding we will need to discuss what we think we mean by the unconscious and what the hidden limitations are in any of the theories we develop about the so-called objective world.

Usually, we make a theory and work on the theory as if it is an objective fact about an objective situation. For instance, while Newton believed he was describing an objective force called gravity, Einstein changed the metaphor and considered gravity as the product of the curvature of space-time. From the Einsteinian perspective, there was no objective single force called "gravity," but rather a condition that manifested through the relationship between several things. This reveals that when we engage in the process of isolating a quality or quantity, believing we have found an "objective" thing, both our naming of the thing and our belief in its objective existence come from our having torn apart some integral system.

Do bacteria cause disease? Or is it a combination of bacteria, internal body enzymes and hormones, cascading chains of reactions, mental attitudes, and emotional conditions? Does chaos exist as an objective condition or does chaos exist only because order exists as well? Does our consciousness actually influence the outcome of quantum experiments, as some theorists have conjectured, or is there some objective state of matter we have just not yet discovered that is doing the work of influencing reality?

Neurobiological research into how memory is contained and communicated in the brain has always focused on the neurons themselves and not on their related structures. Now, however, scientists are beginning to look at the *glial* cells, which hitherto were not considered part of the memory system. As a result, we may soon be thinking of memory as being stored in a much larger portion of the brain, and seeing the brain itself not so much as a neuronal network but as being modeled after an ecology, with all the subtle, self-organizing interrelationships an ecology implies. The point is that it is not simply a matter of new knowledge; rather, our definitions limit our view of reality itself.

Any theory we deal with, no matter how elegant, is not part of the objective world, but what *we* make of this vast, undivided, whole place that we are in from the perspective of little moments of truth: moments that we make into snapshots of this unending, streaming, dynamic wholeness. *What* we make is *who* we are. And *who* we are is *what* we make. In other words, theories are always about ourselves as much as what we are theorizing about.

The same thing is true of psychological theories such as those about the unconscious. I am working under the assumption that, even though there has been much new work since Freud's original conceptualization of the unconscious, some of the basic premises about it have remained fundamentally the same from his time until now. Dreams for Freud were the royal road to the unconscious, and this insight was an auspicious beginning of his attempt to understand this hidden, yet dynamic, aspect of our psyche. He spent the next thirty-odd years describing the territory of this place from an *economic* point of view, meaning from its energy levels, and from a *topographical*, or mapping, point of view.

As a result, the unconscious is typically understood as a psychic location or place that contains in hidden or coded form much of what we need to live a full and satisfying life. Even though we may not articulate it to ourselves, I believe we think of the unconscious as having an *objective* existence. This notion is the first thing I would like to challenge—that is, the idea that there is a *there*, there. Basically, I want to suggest that perhaps our view of the unconscious is something we created and not the unconscious itself. It therefore has embedded in it some of the limitations of who we are as beings. Along with this model's great capacity to visualize some essential truths, it also contains our specific and sometimes narrow point of view.

In developing the psychology of human beings, Freud based many of his assumptions on the existence of drives. While drives do indeed exist, how much of his theoretical thinking was colored by his own psychological needs and the needs of his culture? Indeed, once we see the relative and nonobjective nature of drives, can theoretical structures built around seemingly objective data survive? The important point is that while theories *seem* to be only about the so-called objective world, they are really about the *relationship* between us and this so-called objective world.

Another common understanding is that the unconscious—compared to our conscious state—is somehow *vague* or unclear. A sort of nebulousness is one of its qualities and this characteristic becomes acceptable only as it turns into its opposite: *clarity.*

This unknown area, which is what I am identifying with the unconscious, has in one way or another become for most spiritual seekers the central issue of our lives. Many of us have embarked on a quest to find the Real Self, God, the source of our being, the truth of existence. Whether we call that truth "our relationship with God," "the Real Self," or even "meaning," the unconscious has become like a tower lit with a hazy light that beckons us forward as we try to make sense of things.

Implicit in this model is the statement, "The truth that I need is very far away and it is often mysterious and hidden. It may even be in some sort of a code that I have to interpret and understand. There is a journey that I need to go on to discover myself." Buried just beneath the skin of this statement, however, are many unstated assumptions that we need to examine. To help us understand these assumptions, I would like to briefly introduce the kabbalistic schema of the four universes, a basic statement of universal relationship that will give us a penetrating view into the nature of our relationship with Reality. Investigating the unconscious from this relational perspective will give us deeper insight into what the unconscious really is.

THE FOUR KABBALISTIC UNIVERSES

We could say that from a kabbalistic point of view, understanding the four universes helps us enter a new paradigm of seeing and therefore a new relationship with the world around and within us. Taken together, the four universes—*Assiyah, Yetzirah, Briah,* and *Atzilut*—are a topographical map of Reality. They are a vision of increasing levels of integration: spatially, temporally, physically, psychologically, and spiritually.

> *Assiyah (not Transparent to):*
> > *Yetzirah (not Transparent to):*
> > > *Briah (not Transparent to):*
> > > > *Atzilut (Completely Transparent to):*
> > > *Briah (Transparent to Yetzirah & Assiyah):*
> > *Yetzirah (Transparent only to Assiyah):*
> *Assiyah (not Transparent: sees only itself).*

From Assiyah to Atzilut, the four universes expand in transparency. Here I am using the word *transparent* to mean the quality of allowing Reality, God's totality and presence, to shine through. Assiyah—when looked at from the point of view of its limitations and not its completeness—can see only itself. It is cut off from the Whole. God's Light and consciousness are in their most concealed state, since this universe cannot contain the level of freedom and relationship found in the other universes. In turn, Yetzirah is transparent *only* to Assiyah. We could say that Briah is a state that is transparent to—and therefore includes—the worlds of Yetzirah and Assiyah. Finally, Atzilut—that most essential and integrated state, which is completely transparent to the Heavenly or Unified world—allows us to see that the totality of God is contained in each universe. In other words, the atzilutic understanding of Assiyah is that God is completely and paradoxically present in this very place where the Divine seems most hidden.

An important consideration in thinking about this schema is that, unlike the skins of an onion, these universes are not separate worlds. Instead, each more integrated universe contains the consciousness and conditions found in the less integrated universes. In this way, Yetzirah contains the conditions and understanding of Assiyah, while Briah contains the integration of both Assiyah and Yetzirah, and Atzilut contains Assiyah, Yetzirah, and Briah.

Reality is both *pictured* by and *made* by these levels of self-organizing being and union. By looking through the eyes of this schema we can perceive how our view of reality changes as more and more fragmented parts of ourselves are healed and we become more whole. Through Wholeness we begin to see the world differently. So while time, for example, will flow only from past to future in Assiyah, in Yetzirah, the next most integrated universe, time also flows psychologically—that is, bidirectionally—from past to present and from present to past. In Briah, we encounter time in a state of at-one-ment, a condition almost incomprehensible to assiyatic consciousness.

From a holographic point of view, each human being has access to each of these universes. In fact, it is more accurate to say that—as beings made in the image of our Creator—we *are* all of these universes, though our consciousness may be fixed in one universe more than in another. On the other hand, from the point of view of purification, we must labor to climb the rungs from state to higher state. Both points of view—the linear and the holographic—are true and complementary.

Assiyah

The kabbalistic universe called Assiyah is the universe of *making* or *action*. This universe is the one that is closest to us and our everyday reality. This is the universe where we express ourselves physically and where behavior—*what actually occurs*—is king. This world is tied most closely to the physical in that actions are deeply physical things.

Because the physical realm is so specific and locatable, all the differences between things are highlighted here. Subject and object are clearly delineated and separated. Things that cannot be physically seen or understood, such as the spiritual worlds and God, are believed to be far away, even in physical terms. From an assiyatic point of view, the golden place of unification—Heaven, Shambhala, Shangri-La, Valhalla, Nirvana—is never here; it is always someplace else. Eden is another one of those places we have heard about but can never visit. Everything in Assiyah is about this separation from Eden, which—because our consciousness is not yet whole enough to see God in every physical manifestation—is the basis of our suffering. Assiyah is a world of habit and repetition. If there were an assiyatic therapeutic approach to life, it would be based on a behaviorist model; feelings and interior states are not considered. All we need to do is figure out what the behavior is we want to change, and then find the way to make it happen. As we all know, this approach can sometimes be very valuable.

In the world of Assiyah the ego is at its densest. We fully and firmly believe that we are *somebody,* and we never question the rightness of this view. And even though we believe we are somebody, we are not concerned with the inner self very much because there is not so much of an inner self here. We are more concerned with how this self makes its way in the world: who supports its existence and desires and who stands in the way. From this perspective, the world is essentially divided.

This assiyatic universe is influenced by brute force and magic. Brute force speaks for itself: Assiyah is the universe of war. In Assiyah there is a gulf between us and the unseen, an abyss between us and the world, but the world of spirit still influences us. Seen from an assiyatic perspective, the only way to bridge the separation and communicate with the unseen world that has power over us is through magic and ritual. Although we don't quite understand how what we do travels through the air, so to speak, to the world of spirit, we become involved in a sort of magical thinking. We promote the magical view of the world and use some form of magic, including drawings, spells, idols, and, most important, charisma and glamour, to communicate with, effect change in, and placate this unseen world that we sense—almost fearfully—is there. We know this is vitally important to our souls and to our way of life. So Assiyah is basically a superstitious place.

Because of this type of thinking, in Assiyah we have totems, objects that convey power, whether it be a fancy car or a powerful husband for a woman, a beautiful or powerful woman for a man, a beautiful man for a woman, or a famous or glamorous lover. The possibilities are endless. If the thing is not seen for itself, but for what it conveys about the so-called owner of that object, then that thing is a magical thing, a totem. When we make any integral, whole thing—whether it is a person or an object—into a totem, we are in a sense denying its reality and using it to relate to a portion or part of ourselves. Making a person or object unreal, with no intrinsic content, also has the effect of making us less real, as we pull ourselves out of Wholeness in order to accentuate a portion of our totality.

Totems become the objective repository of our inner psychology, thereby "solving" the assiyatic problem of having an interior psychology that is vague and confused, and whose very existence makes us uncomfortable. Since Assiyah is dedicated to seeing the world in a purely objective way, without the participation of any interior psychology, we don't place the ego in interior space. The ego is someplace "out there," between us and the world. It is what mediates between *us* and the *world*. This arrangement is very primitive, and we might say that certain aspects of Assiyah are pre-egoic.

One of my favorite philosophers, Jean Gebser, notes in his book *The Ever-Present Origin* that: "all magic, even today, occurs in the natural, vital, egoless, spaceless and timeless sphere. That sphere . . . is not a transcendental sphere but a pre-egoic sphere. It hasn't gotten to that. This requires, as far as present-day man is concerned, a sacrifice of consciousness. It occurs in the state of trance or when the consciousness dissolves."

Following Gebser, we can say that in Assiyah, there is not a lot of consciousness. The discontinuity between inside and outside—while Assiyah remains unredeemed by the understanding evoked by the other, more essential universes of Yetzirah and Briah—is so complete as to be profound.

Yetzirah

The next universe, Yetzirah, makes a quantum leap into a new, exciting, and powerful paradigm. In Yetzirah we discover the world of internal feelings and even the staggering concept that this whole interior world is for us an undiscovered country. We begin to see that we have fears and longings, and we begin to get hints about how much we do not know about ourselves and the world. In yetziratic consciousness we begin to look for the origin of our feelings. This journey can at times be terrifying. Because of our awareness of desire, we now have a different relationship with the world. We begin to see both our known and unknown internal desires as the lens through which we see the world.

In Assiyah, in its pure, unrelated, or cut-off form, we don't understand that we see through a *personal* lens. We believe that the world is a certain way and that we are a certain way, and that is that. In Yetzirah, we are not so sure. A level of certainty has disintegrated. Now, for the first time, we begin to see how we participate in the making of the world. We have good days; we have bad days; and we begin to see that this doesn't only have to do with the barometric pressure or whether it's sunny or gray. It doesn't only have to do with somebody smiling at us or not smiling at us. It doesn't only have to do with whether our husband, wife, mate, or partner was nice to us the night before. Instead, there is now a psychic center, an interior self that reflects upon things and understands that "I (my interior self) goes through something." We start saying, "What am I going through? Why am I going through this stuff?" This is a considerable paradigm shift from the assiyatic view where everything is oriented outward.

Freud's psychology—primarily driven by the desires that he called drives—is firmly the invention or view of reality from this universe. It is interesting to note that as the movement toward psychological awareness took hold in people's imaginations, spirits, and bodies, there was less and less room for a connection to something called "God." There was less and less room for a God that was not seen as a projection of inner needs. In fact, Freud called the need for religion a remnant of childhood helplessness. For somebody who is firmly anchored in a solely yetziratic position, that is true.

We begin to see the powerful truth of this paradigm and start believing that *this* is the only reality, *this* is the way that things work. We get to a new rung on the ladder and set up shop, believing we have found "the truth," that *this* is it. To a yetziratically astute person—one who is psychologically aware and grounded—someone who is caught up in the drama of Assiyah would seem very limited.

Subject and object in Yetzirah are still separate as they are in Assiyah, but no longer in such a hard-and-fast way. For instance, in Assiyah, we were part of a community. But this was a community, a race or tribe, specifically connected by physical attributes. In yetziratic consciousness, on the other hand, the definition of who is part of our tribe enlarges. We now see our connection with other people who have similar *feelings* as ourselves. They could be from many different tribes, but they are part of our tribe because they participate in the same awareness that we do.

The yetziratic quest to live a fuller life takes on a very different form from the assiyatic quest. We become a tribe of archaeologists of feeling who search for hidden motivations and look for the enduring presence of the past in our present life. Yetzirah is map making. We want to learn to make the map that we need to follow on our path into the unknown so that we can live more satisfying, more whole, more complete lives. Spiritual work, when seen as a quest for knowledge, connection, or enlightenment, is primarily a yetziratic endeavor.

In Yetzirah we travel into the unknown in order to bring out the prize. The prize is finding God. The prize is enlightenment. The prize is awakening. The prize is meaning. I am sure there are as many names for the prize as there are people in the world, but the sense of what I am saying still applies. The search for the spiritual prize is the work of spirit from a yetziratic point of view.

In Yetzirah the ego is centrally located in the psyche, and it is the seat of the personal "I am" consciousness. However, it is softened somewhat from the hard perspective of Assiyah; it changes from being very dense to become a more fluid thing. Instead of just encompassing us, it encompasses a *portion* of the world and a *portion* of us. It encompasses our genetic and cultural inheritance, our received view, and our personally generated view.

In the yetziratic state, one still believes oneself to be *somebody*, to be a separate individual. This separate individual is searching for what he or she recognizes as some sort of implicit connection with the All, with the universe. This is an individual who lives and dies, who is born in mystery and lives and dies in mystery, who must go on a vision quest of some sort or follow a path in order to find Wholeness.

Another fundamental quality of the yetziratic ego is that it is completely self-reflective: it knows itself only by looking at itself. While individuals whose consciousness is fixed solely in Assiyah never look at themselves in a deep way—knowing themselves only by looking outward at the world—in Yetzirah we know ourselves by reflecting upon our own existence. In Yetzirah, reflecting upon life becomes as important as participating in it. In Assiyah, how we *acted* determined who we felt ourselves to be; in Yetzirah, what we *feel* about ourselves and our actions is how we define ourselves.

In order to exist, the yetziratic ego needs to stand a little apart, witnessing the drama, commenting on it to itself in order to understand it better. Of course, it itself has created this drama of separateness by standing apart. The ego therefore looks at itself and finds in its perception of separateness a true picture of the world, forgetting for the moment that it is not looking at the world but at itself. This remarkable state of affairs is the situation in which we all find ourselves.

Briah

Briah is the highly integrated universe of creation, which contains the consciousness of both Assiyah and Yetzirah. This universe stands at the interface of Oneness and Separateness. It is the truth of our Oneness with the Creator and the truth of our individual existence and responsibility, the "oneness of Oneness and the oneness of Duality." From the perspective of Briah, Yetzirah—despite all its sophistication—still looks profoundly limited. The whole of Yetzirah and Assiyah taken together can be seen for the first time for what it really is: fiction. It is fiction because it is only part of the picture, and we tend to identify with it as a picture of the Whole. Briah is the realm of "is-ness," wherein each thing—free of the objectification of Assiyah and the historical, psychological pain of Yetzirah—is finally completely itself and thus shines with the Light of God.

From the perspective of the small self, everything is a problem; but from a briatic point of view, it is not. For example: from the perspective of the small "I," making an autonomous, self-actualized statement can lead to danger, for "they" may not like it. This can lead to even more danger: "They may abandon me and I will be left to suffer desolate aloneness." Obviously, in this case autonomous action brings out the memory of past events—which are yetziratic in origin. But from the perspective of Briah, autonomy is one of the pure, actualized, real, and God-given states. There is no question but that the self *is* autonomous, that even as it is part of everything, it simultaneously stands alone. Paradox is no problem in Briah.

The ego, on the other hand, cannot abide this paradox and splits into two. Not only does the ego look at itself to see how it is doing in this circumstance, but it splits even further into "itself" and "the other," in this case, the people who will—transferentially—"abandon one for being oneself."

The ego's agony is that it is always split. Its nature is separateness, and all it sees is the distance of the long journey home. From the perspective of Briah, one eventually sees the ego—with all its convolutions—and the Real Self as exactly the same thing. From that perspective, there is only one "I Am." The nature of this deeper "I Am," the "I" of the "I," which we encounter for the first time in Briah, is that it encompasses all opposites and sees them as dualistic expressions of a unified thing.

While many people have touched pieces of the freedom that comes with the consciousness of this universe, Briah can also be approached as a kind of defense against the pain of living, a kind of dissociation for the purposes of protection against the difficulties of life. Embodied fully, however—meaning that it does not split from the universes of Assiyah and Yetzirah, which are part of its makeup—Briah offers the chance to live a completely human life, with the suffering inherent in being a separate human being *and* the joy of knowing that we are, as each created thing is, part of God's creative activity.

Atzilut

Atzilut is the most essential, or most deeply integrated, of the kabbalistic universes. It is the universe that is most transparent to God's Light, having never been shattered during the process of Creation. In other words, Atzilut is so integrated that it provides little barrier to the essential truth of God's world. It is completely absorbed in the Divine milieu. From the linear or hierarchical point of view, this universe is almost unreachable by our current possible level of purification. From the holographic point of view, however, it is not so much *reachable*—as the potential linear product of purification—as "possible to manifest"—as a state of surrender and grace. When we go full circle in the spiritual journey, we find that God was never far from us, but closer than we could ever imagine. When our lives are fully filled with this completion, and when we begin to live this truth with other people—seeing them as they are, sharing and using our knowledge to bring our fellow beings to the root of their being and therefore into relationship with God—we might be said to be living an atzilutic life, the life of *healing* and *return*.

Atzilut is the end of the journey, the final understanding of the fact that God is fully here, that there was never any separate place to go. As such, the realm of Atzilut is beyond description: it is the world, ourselves, our consciousness itself. It is the "world to come," here and now. While it can be experienced, to talk about it creates a "thing-ness" that is not part of its nature.

THE UNCONSCIOUS AND THE SEARCH FOR MEANING

Although all four universes are our birthright, we live most of our lives as if it were truly possible to live in a portion of reality. When the originally unified ground of being pokes its head into the dualistic, less integrated worlds of Yetzirah and Assiyah, these states—which are unified in Briah—appear split and paradoxical. In other words, this paradox is what some deeper, unified truth looks like from the egoic, objectified—and therefore split—view.

In physics, this paradox shows up in the dual nature of quantum matter as wave and particle. In philosophy, it shows up as the concept of *vagueness,* the study of which has become a discipline unto itself. *Vagueness* shows us that many of the concepts we take for granted cannot be quantified. For instance, we all know what *tall* means, but exactly when does tall start? At five feet six inches? Seven inches? Ten inches? We all know what a heap of sand looks like, but how many grains make a heap? When do grains of sand suddenly become a heap and when, by taking grains away, does it cease being a heap?

This ambiguity—which is a true feature of the world—appears in the self-reflective world as the opposing states of psychological reality. Our reaction to this reality is the borderline dilemma in all of us, the conflict between self and other, between our existence and the threats of the world, the misunderstandings of where our self and the selves of others start and stop.

We can gain a deeper understanding of this dilemma and the way out by a close examination of the consciousness of Yetzirah as it looks from a briatic position, shown by the diagrams below.

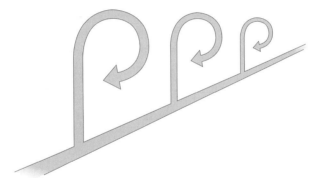

Figure 1.1. An example of three individual consciousnesses.

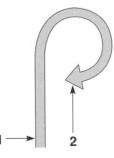

Figure 1.2. 1 = individual consciousness; 2 = the bending of that consciousness as it becomes self-aware.

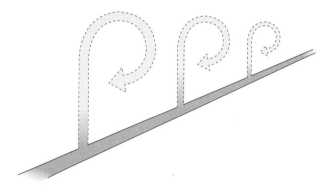

Figure 1.3. Seemingly individual consciousnesses arise from a current that is not personally owned.

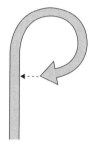

Figure 1.4. The search for meaning.

In the first diagram, the curved arrow shapes represent our individual selves.

In the second diagram, the parts of the individual consciousness are made plain. Numeral 1 is the individual consciousness and numeral 2 represents the bending of that consciousness as it becomes self-aware.

The third diagram highlights the fact that all of these seemingly individual consciousnesses arise from a current that is not personally owned.

The final diagram indicates how the individual consciousness—unknowingly looking back at itself—sees in that distance the object of its desire for unification. The search for meaning that arises in the gap between the seer and the seen becomes the spiritual path itself, specifically that stage of the path in which one identifies oneself as a *seeker*, one who is on a quest to find the truth.

Although we experience ourselves as having separate domains of consciousness, from the perspective of Briah, there is only one source of consciousness. As a paraphrase of the Shema (the supreme statement of faith in the Oneness of God in the Jewish liturgy) might put it: "Listen, you who are trying to make sense of what Reality is from the perspective of the separate self: Reality is Unified."

When we identify ourselves as the ego—only a part of our individual consciousness, represented by the *tip* of the arrow in the second figure—there seem to be "two." When we return to the root of the separate "I," which would be like moving counterclockwise from the arrow tip of the diagram back around to its origin, we see that there is only one source of consciousness, which often looks at the individualized self.

The unconscious exists as a device or state only from the perspective of the arrow's tip, which is cut off from knowledge of its true shape and origin and looks across an imagined gulf to find its real self. We split off from this true self from the moment we look at our own consciousness. We imagine that we *are* that "tip," and therefore there are many things in the world that seem to threaten our continued existence as separate individuals.

For example, if someone told us that we were worthless, that would be a threat to the separate ego. On the other hand, if someone told us that our hard-won ego was really an illusion, that too would be threatening. Anything that threatened the status quo, the ego's controlled view of things, would be seen as a dire threat. The truth, however, is more startling: if we continue our search to the root of consciousness, we see that this root is not personally owned. Rather, it is held in common by *all* manifestation. There is no one to whom consciousness "belongs." This is the theme of the third figure.

If the notion, implications, and manifestation of the egoic self change from universe to universe, what does the unconscious look like as we get increasingly whole? As we become more and more integrated? Remember that in Yetzirah the ego-function from the perspective of the tip of the arrow is to know, and "to know" is the ego's greatest mission and challenge. The need to know something implies that there is something important that is not known, something that is not under the ego's control. What is not known to the ego, the ego terms "the unconscious," and its content is seen as the great object of desire of the infinitely deep yetziratic consciousness. For the yetziratic ego, the unconscious is the Holy Grail. It is Mecca. It is the Garden of Eden. It is the palace of enlightenment. The search for meaning that arises in this way is the spiritual path itself.

Seeing the unconscious as the reservoir of the *unknown-which-needs-to-become-known* is an invention of the egoic self-identity that arises in Yetzirah. The ego creates the unconscious and the unconscious creates the ego. They are mutually co-arising. In Yetzirah you cannot talk about one without the other. From a kabbalistic point of view, the ego or the self-identity is the maker of the theory of the unconscious as a reservoir for the unknown or as the location of that unknown, and the desire to make that unknown known.

When we are entranced in the self-reflective model of the self, then *meaning* is the most important thing. The search for meaning, and along with it the "spiritual quest"—when tied to the needs of the ego to know itself—is a powerful motivator that moves the individual to seek the truth. The ego, in other words, is the helper who teaches us to search beneath appearances.

This search eventually comes to an end, however. It gets used up. It gets old, stale. At some point, it no longer works. And then something else is needed. This is the view from Briah. Up until the point at which the search gets stale, the unconscious was the object of this search, psychologically seen as the place where the hidden dynamics of life were kept, and metaphorically seen as unknown, which the ego spent its time trying to make known.

A new approach is now called for—especially since the centralized, self-reflecting ego is no longer solely in charge. We know "the looker," the witness, is at the end of what it can see. In Briah, the unconscious is seen as the Unmanifest or Absolute and takes on an entirely new meaning. Then the arrow tip and the arrow itself are seen as the same thing; the spiritual quest and its resolution are seen as the same thing. Search is no longer opposed to not-search. You do what you want and what you want to do is what you must do.

In Briah, all is hidden and all is simply flow. Here the unconscious retains its mystery and has no mystery at all. Here it is the object of the quest and the vehicle that we ride to any place that we choose. And strangely enough, when we are that free, we all choose to ride to one place, which is to God's home.

This home is the place where we have utter free will and the freedom to realize that we have no free will at all, that we are made of God stuff looking at God stuff. Then it is not so terrible that we are these egos bent back looking at ourselves. It is God looking at God. It is not a big deal. It is nothing to be ashamed of. It is nothing to be caught by. It is a wonderful thing.

One of the hallmarks of Briah consciousness is that each thing is itself. This "itself" in Zen Buddhism is called "is-ness" or *fu-e-go*. Here is Zen teacher Suzuki-roshi talking about this idea:

[T]he usual person sticks to *ji*, "things." That is quite usual. Characteristic of Buddha's teaching is to go beyond "things.". . . [W]hen we go beyond the subjective and objective world, beyond *ji*, we come to understand oneness of everything, oneness of subjectivity and objectivity, oneness of inside and outside . . . each one of us is the boss of the whole world. . . . We are independent, each one of us is completely independent, absolutely independent. There is nothing to compare with you. You are you, just you. We have to understand things in both ways. One is interrelated, to understand things as interrelated being. The other way is to understand ourselves as quite independent from everything. When we include everything we are completely independent because there is nothing left to compare with you. (From *Wind Bell*/San Francisco Zen Center)

While in Yetzirah the unconscious becomes a gateway to Reality, from the perspective of Briah, it is a dynamic gateway to Reality as well as Reality Itself, without the need to reveal or explain. From a briatic point of view, the unconscious is a gateway not because it illuminates us, that is, the "us" of the self-reflective model, but because it is, as we are, independent and interrelated at the same time. It is the "I am" of both the small egoic consciousness and the ground of being that we all share in common. In its great silence it holds our connection to the sacred All.

The unconscious in Briah is neither personal nor impersonal. It is also not bound by time or space. The important point here is that even though the truth of Briah is hidden from us in yetziratic consciousness, or, put another way, even though our yetziratic mentality is not transparent to Briah, and briatic truth cannot shine through to our consciousness, it is nevertheless true. And while it is true that we cannot learn to be One until our egos are strong enough to let us be separate, we also need to know we *are* One before we truly can be separate.

Separateness becomes simply the play of the Divine in the manifest world, each created thing a thing-in-itself that sings God's praise. It is all of the things-in-themselves playing with each other. It is an ordinary thing. It is the sunlight falling on the dust of pollen, and it is bees carrying pollen to other plants. It is soil being created from things that died, and it is new things growing. It is the astounding sentence of life.

The unconscious in Briah is also nonlocal. It is not personally owned. Its existence not only results from the view from divided human perception, but is intrinsic to the origination of matter itself, as matter's appearance splits the singular plenum into two things. In fact, consciousness—and with it the unconscious—is not even owned by human beings. It is not limited to human beings. It is not a human archetype that we human beings hold together by our existence. Stones have it; pollen has it; seas have it; trees have it; birds have it; fish have it, all in different ways. It is nonlocal all-at-one-ment. It is not our personal domain. Because of the truth of this, every once in a while we see the world for what it is: a shimmering eternity in the face of time, or a shining moment in Eternity.

The briatic view—which can be glimpsed only to the extent that we have reconciled ourselves with our histories through yetziratic work—is seen to be truly nondual, which means that it is *not* not-personal and *not* not-impersonal. It is this understanding that lets us touch God's Hand.

Even if we haven't personally experienced the unconscious from a briatic point of view, even if we are not living it consciously at the moment, it is still going on; it is still the truth. Even if we are only beginning to understand this truth intellectually, it is going on. Because this view from Briah is true, it has implications even for the deep yetziratic work of depth psychology, for instance. It is important for us to know about this state of being because without it we have only a portion of the truth, thinking that we are separate beings; that small perspective limits our ability to help. As people who help others and work on ourselves, the suffering we face is the drama of this separateness.

It is in Briah that we learn about the Unmanifest's power to embrace our life with its final meaning. We understand that there was never any place to go, that there was never any place that we came from, that there is no coming and going. When we begin to experience that, a deep relaxation begins to take hold of us. That relaxation lets us participate in life and lets life flow through us in a way that was impossible from the tense position of the one who quests in Yetzirah. This allows us to live and not hold back. It allows us to be fully committed and take full responsibility joyfully.

In Briah, the experience of the unconscious becomes pure presence or pure participation, the origin of the felt sense of Presence, the origin place of meaning, the meta-place of meaning, the cleaving to God *and* God, the act and the non-act. In Briah we learn how to be born over and over again as we watch the wind in the trees and know, "This is our self." In Briah we learn how to die as we watch the wind wane and the trees crumble to dust, and know, "This is also our self."

One of my colleagues and students, Dr. Martha Harrell, put it this way in a recent letter to me. I quote:

As I've been wandering in this place of Briah, it seems to me that a new way can open for me, maybe for us all. Not to have to go the way of suffering. I mean to not seek the cause and motivations of everything as we do in Yetzirah, but to let the mystery live and go the way of offering. By that I mean to be alert and modest, not careless or hypervigilant and to fill ourselves up in this strange place so that the overflow pours out onto others. . . . So we give to others not by sacrifice (as in the traditional view of therapy where the therapist sacrifices his or her own needs and feelings for the sake of the patients) but from the overflow of our own fullness. In this way it is not a choice between opposites—my benefit or yours—but we all receive the EverFlow.

We need to think about this. We need to be brave so that we can go through whatever we have to go through to experience this God-given state of being that allows us to do the work of true transformation for ourselves and others, now seen for the first time as separate and non-separate simultaneously. We need to be able to invite *Yichida,* the unique, Intimate One, into our hearts and be filled with the glow of the undivided consciousness that God gave us to have and hold, married to it with our bodies and minds.

QUESTIONS AND ANSWERS

Question: I was wondering if you could say a little more about the ego as being the result of matter coming into existence.

Jason: Actually, what I said was that the unconscious is the result of matter coming into existence. The whole drama arises from that primal moment: as soon as we look at ourselves, we have to bend our neck, so to speak. If we have to bend our neck to look at ourselves, certain muscles (metaphorically) are going to be used; certain muscles are not going to be used; certain muscles may be strained; certain muscles are not going to be strained. So as soon as we decide to look at ourselves, or as soon as looking—and therefore separation—happens, a whole causal series is set in motion. The very act of the Unmanifest manifesting creates the whole drama of duality. Then any possible manifestation would show two faces. In Briah, they are two faces of one being. In Yetzirah and Assiyah, they are two separate things and are often at odds with each other. But in Briah we have the body-sense, the grounded spiritual sense, of being a third thing that is the origin of both of these apparent faces or opposites.

We could also say, just as you did, that the ego's coming into existence is simultaneous with matter's coming into existence. Before matter, there was no direction, no up or down, north or south. But as soon as there is matter, there is *place*. The jump from "place" to "*my* place" is easy to see!

Question: I have always thought that when we die, we are going to know what God's plan is, that we are going to be let in on the secret.

Jason: Probably everybody in this room has had that notion. It is the final hope of the yetziratic and assiyatic ego that when it dies, whatever that means, the plan will be revealed to us, as if we step out of who we have been for all of our lives and see the plan stretched before us from some serene vantage point. This notion can be sustained only by the suffering, separate ego that sees itself and its existence as still separate from God and the Universe, and, even as it wants some form of "eternal life," suffers because of its loneliness. From this position, we look to death as a kind of savior that will do what we couldn't do for ourselves: stop our usual thinking process so that we can actually finally figure out what is going on. You know a plant doesn't figure out how to move this way or that way to follow the sun. Instead it is phototropic. It has one rule that God gave it: *you shall love the sun.* That is its nature, and following its nature, it follows the sun. So the plant is not separate from the sun at all. Since the sun and the plant are bound by love, there is never any question of separation. There is never a question of the plant having to know anything. After we die, we continue to be what we always were at heart: love itself.

I'll ask you a question in return: What do you think this plan would look like if you were not separate from it? As we integrate our consciousness more and more, some questions drop away, and this is one of them. From an integrated perspective, we need to be asking this question every minute, not from a sense of fear, but from the joyous announcement of purpose. We should ask, "What does God want of me now? How should my Real Self realize itself in this moment?" The answer to *that* is God's plan.

Question: In order to get deeply into the unified state you are calling Briah, it seems that you have to devote your entire life to it and remove yourself from regular life, drop everything and become a monk. Is this necessary?

Jason: A good question. Two things are simultaneously true. The first is that it takes complete commitment to find and live in unified or related consciousness. You are absolutely right in saying that it seems to take the constancy and dedication of a monk, someone who is totally devoted to finding the truth, to listening to God's voice. And I hope that one of the things I can do is to encourage people to be that devoted.

But it is simultaneously true that God does not insist on any particular approach. One of the things God provides us with, along with life itself, is the Attribute of Mercy. This means that there are many, many ways to see God. One of those ways is through family; other ways are through helping others, through cooking, through marriage, through working at a job, and so on. Life itself is the great teacher. If God has provided that life can take you all of the way to the state that I am talking about, then it is just a matter of living your life and paying exquisite attention.

Now we are into a different kind of thinking; we have a new perspective. When you have a relationship with a husband or wife or partner, and both of you are completely devoted to this awareness, this holy work, then you are going to watch carefully the hologram of that relationship, and you will find that everything you need to know is there. Looking in your children's eyes; watching them go to school; fearing for their safety; watching them get sick and get well; watching them grow and leave you: all of these different things are in the hologram of life.

I am a great believer in God. I am a great believer that God did not require that Awakening or Wholeness be available only to people who had enough money to be in therapy or who were lucky enough to live in peaceful times, or only to those who were Jews or Christians or Muslims or Hindus or Buddhists. We are very lucky if we find our way to such a path. Having these tools, these revelations, helps us to speed up our development tremendously. But life, it seems to me, is the one great teacher. It is God's greatest gift. One of Judaism's great lessons is the notion that essentially there is no division between Heaven and Earth. According to the kabbalistic saying "As above, so below," Heaven needs to be found right here on Earth. And when we find our life here on Earth, when we realize it completely, when we accept the duality of life with exquisite attention and devotion, we find Heaven as well. Life is God's ultimate answer to our questions.

Question: Do only human beings self-reflect? Does that mean that animals don't? Or that they just don't bother to do that sort of thing?

Jason: I can answer that from the graduated and hierarchical point of view or the holographic point of view. From the hierarchical view we would probably say that rocks, trees, and animals have not yet reached the level of freedom and self-responsibility that exists in the truly self-reflective universe of Yetzirah. In the hierarchical point of view there is a difference between us and a stone or us and an animal. So from that point of view we would have to say that humans are somewhat higher, somewhat closer to Heaven, and therefore have more choices and more responsibility. From another point of view, there is a lot to learn from a rock. I had a rock outside my office, which I decided to carve. I bought tools and I decided to make a trough so that it would collect rainwater and I could put a little Buddha next to it and maybe a little flower to float in it after it rained. So I had this piece of New Jersey granite and it decided to be completely unworkable. What that meant was that after three weeks of hitting it with chisels and a three-pound hammer, I have a trough about three-quarters of an inch deep.

So what I am learning about this rock is that the trough is going to come when I surrender various things. For instance, it is going to appear when I surrender the notion of beginning and ending, because this may take a long time. It is going to come when I give up the notion of beauty and nonbeauty, hard and soft. For instance, beginning to carve again this season, I've learned to hit the stone a lot softer. It turns out that when I hit the stone softly, but at the correct angle, the flakes fall away much faster.

So this rock is teaching me, from the holographic point of view, enormous lessons. You may think that it is *me* who is teaching *me*, but that is not so. It is rock-consciousness. It is God in the stone.

Question: To be within the briatic world . . .

Jason: Which means to be in the yetziratic and assiyatic worlds as well . . .

Question: . . . the way we achieve that level, it is a static phenomenon. Static in the sense that you are part of it and it is revolving around and you are not separate from it. You are part of it but it is just there. You don't have to make any effort to be there.

Jason: Not true. And I could have said true just as well. Here we are in paradoxical language. There is enormous effort involved here: every minute *kavannah* (intention). So it takes tremendous effort to *not-do*. And this not-doing is very different from the assiyatic not-doing, which is about not putting out effort or ignoring.

Comment: In fact, isn't it true that if there is effort, that is a negation of that unified reality?

Jason: Correct, and yet both effort and noneffort have to be accomplished. This is about choiceless-choice, effortless-effort. Do you hear what I'm saying? In Briah, the work of Yetzirah goes on. The work of Assiyah goes on. We are beholden to call upon the greatest courage in ourselves—our highest fortitude, our deepest longing—to do this work so that we can help ourselves and the world. Our ability to help grows to the extent that we are one with our true self, the self God made in God's image. This is not the Oneness that denies duality, but the Oneness that embraces it. This is briatic consciousness. It is our ability to look at both sides of creation and see the Face of God. Then we dwell in God's house, happy to find that it was our home all along.

T W O

Living between the Light and Dark: The Holy Ego

The individual self is part of who we are, and it is only a problem if we do not see all of who we are as holy. If we see all as holy, then we do our best to heal the extreme separateness the ego has fallen into because of the wounds of our karma, culture, childhood, and civilization, and the existential problems of life itself.

APPROACHING GOD

LIVING AS WE DO, between Heaven and Earth, the spiritual path has never been an easy one. With so many approaches to the task of "finding God" created over so long a period, you would think that there would be some consensus about how to handle the difficult challenge of relating to the human personality and its problems.

The truth, however, is very different. Not only is there no consensus, but instead, spiritual paths have divided pretty much along two main approaches, both hoping to deal with the problem of duality and Oneness and where the human ego fits into this scheme.

The first approach, the one most of us here in the West grew up with, is the theistic or deistic path. This understanding places the Deity outside the person. It asks individuals to find the will of God and, to the best of their ability, follow the path that brings them closer to their Creator.

In this approach to the Divine, the spiritual path is a heroic one wherein the seeker goes through various tests in order to finally meet the Deity in some manner or at least know God's will. The deistic way is one of purifying the ego so that the personality is "pure enough" to be with the exemplar of purity, God.

In the final analysis, this path is one of embodiment on the one hand and surrender on the other. One must first take the ego or personality in hand and subdue the wild tiger of the self, while building up the stamina and bravery needed for the journey. Finally, one surrenders the ego to the greater good of God. In this path, we are called upon to reach closeness with the source of our being by following a prescribed path of commandments, ways of being laid out by God and transmitted to us by the prophets in texts such as the Jewish Torah, the Christian New Testament, the Islamic Koran, and others.

By using the example of the most rigorous version of this path—the orthodox or fundamentalist point of view—we can make two general statements about this approach. First, it asserts that the truth has been revealed and can be found outside the self and followed in order to reach God. Second, it claims that the ego-personality or personal self ultimately needs to be surrendered to the Deity in order for the seeker to find the "peace that passeth understanding."

The other main approach might be called the nontheistic, *advaitic,* or nondual approach. In this approach, God is not considered to be something separate at all. Instead, the personal ego is regarded as an illusion that one must see through in order to come to an understanding of the basic ground of being beneath appearances.

In these paths, rigor is used to see through the identification of the self with both personal behavior and even the body itself. These paths presuppose that the truthful layer of understanding is already there; the way must simply be cleared so that the truth can be seen. So these nondual paths are not so much paths of *purification* as paths of *being,* where the truth of who we are is found by inquiry of some sort, such as meditation practices that help us see through the static of the mind to the essential nature of life that was there all along.

These two paths use different language to describe the achievement each recommends. The deistic paths speak of saints, God-cleaving, revelation, and illumination, and the nondual paths speak of self-realization, enlightenment, and awakening.

It is my belief that the possible distortions inherent in both these approaches—and certainly in the way they have been communicated—attempt to erase the very vehicle that allows us to live as divine creations.

THE HEALED EGO

The vehicle that enables us to live as who we are—that is, as individual personalities in finite bodies who are *simultaneously* manifestations of Spirit beyond life and death—is the human ego. While problematic in its unhealed state, the ego in its healed state is the best vehicle we have for bringing us to the gate of enlightenment. To that end, I would like to describe a different approach to working with the ego, in which the personal self is not seen as the antagonist of self-realization or a life devoted to God. In this view, we go beyond the concept of an enemy and find Wholeness where it already exists: in the human ego, which allows for both self-realization and God-connectedness. From this perspective, enlightenment is a form of nonviolence to all, including one's own ego.

However, the usual understanding of the God-awakened or enlightened state is that it is a condition that seems to posit no personal self, but only some sort of "transcendental view" in which the person who has come into the light of understanding or the Light of God is connected to something so great that it makes the ego pale in its light. In this view—found in both the advaitic/nondual and theistic models—the ego is a kind of enemy. In the advaitic context the ego must be seen through; in the theistic, it must be conquered. This is a misunderstanding of what enlightenment or awakening into God actually is.

A quote from the Dalai Lama points to a problem that arises from this view of enlightenment. Here His Holiness is describing a form of compassion that is not based in any way on the needs or attitudes of the one who is feeling compassion. In fact, this teacher feels that when the personal self is involved in any way, compassion in its highest form has not yet come into being.

> Compassion without attachment is possible. Therefore, we need to clarify the distinctions between compassion and attachment. True compassion is not just an emotional response but a firm commitment founded in reason. Because of this firm foundation, a truly compassionate attitude toward others does not change even if they behave negatively. Genuine compassion is based not on our own projections and expectations, but rather on the needs of the other. . . . This is genuine compassion . . . the goal is to develop this genuine compassion, this genuine wish for the well-being of another.

My problem here is not with the end point or desired result of this compassion. It is with the implied methodology. The Dalai Lama recommends practices that are altruistic, which do not highlight or support the ego, but help to diminish its central position in the human psyche. Here it might be construed that the Buddhist belief is that the human attachment to the "I," or the very existence of the personal self, inhibits openness to others, and that only by seeing through the seeming solidity of the "I-thought" can the nondual enlightened life be approached. There are similar examples in the deistic path that take the same point of view from the opposite end of the tunnel. The testament of Christ, for example, is filled with Jesus' selfless actions, and it is his selflessness that is mostly held up for emulation.

Yet practitioners of both of these approaches who have achieved Wholeness do not seem to be selfless or colorless people. Instead, they seem to be vivid personalities who know what they want and what they do not want, who stand for what they believe in, even unto death.

It is clear from this that it is not the ego per se that has either been purified away or seen through, but the unhealthy ego. It is vital that we differentiate between these two aspects of the human psyche, since it will give us a way to work with ourselves that will allow us to avoid falling into the error of trying to pretend to be what we are not: trying to be "self-less," when every atom in our body wants to have a self; trying to be altruistic and override our own needs while these needs are overwhelming and powerful. This behavior sets up a dichotomy between self and other and cannot be seen as nonviolent. It says, for instance, that something of our own self must be lowered or sacrificed in order to be of true service to others, that lowering ourselves and service to others are linked concepts.

Is it not possible for a healthy or healed ego to be compassionate in a nondual way? In a way that includes self and other? Is it even possible that this is the *function* of the healed ego, that is, to be of service to self and other *simultaneously?*

To approach the spiritual life without this understanding is to think that we must destroy what God made: an individual. It means we have not yet found a way to see the holiness of creation in a completely nonviolent manner, a manner in which even the ego is not "killed" in order for it to heal. The need to kill, subjugate, or ignore the ego for some "higher purpose" leads to problems down the line and could even be said to have brought us to the desperate conditions we find our world in today.

THE DESIRE TO EXIST

So what exactly is this ego that can sometimes appear in a healthy state and sometimes in an unhealthy state? That can be both an impediment to awakening and not an impediment, at exactly the same time? While we usually think of the ego as a psychological component of the individual human being, we might redefine it here for the purposes of our discussion as *the very desire to exist,* and in that way see it as a universal quality that is beyond the "human-only" in that it is found in some form or other in every created thing. It appears in the Nothingness of the Absolute and divides the universe into where "we" are and where "we" are not. We could even go so far as to say that before this division, there is no "universe." And by "we" I mean not only humans, but rather all things: *here* is a proton, *there* is a neutron, and in this way of perceiving we see the Creation of the world as an act of separation.

The ego is a demarcation that says, "I exist," or even, "Existence is!" It separates the Absolute into foreground and background and creates—eventually, and many steps removed—the human psychological qualities of conscious self-reflection and the unconscious self, since what is known and what is unknown arise together as one unit, through the same single action.

Kabbalists use the term Ayn-Sof to speak of Divinity that is beyond manifestation and nonmanifestation, foreground and background. The term God and the various Names of God (such as Adonai, Elohim, Yah, and others, which are sometimes used in kabbalistic study as a methodology for unifying consciousness) are reserved for the Godhead associated with manifestation, or Creation. From that perspective, we might say that God's Ego—the Primary Desire to Exist—created the world and is manifestation itself. Thus God's Ego is the model for what the healed ego is.

This divine and healthy model of Creation *must automatically* create opposites, since embedded within the very notion of Creation is the act of separating one thing from another. Though the products of this activity of division seem to be in opposition, they really have a common origin in the act of creation. In this way we can say that the conditions of the entire world are mutually co-arising. On the deepest level, the creation of opposites is not in itself a problem.

When we draw a line on a blank piece of paper, we automatically create *two* worlds: the place the line *is* and the blank space where the line *isn't*, the fullness of the line and the emptiness of the unmarked space. It is the same with the world. Every act of creation makes the world dual: *hot* is responsible for the existence of *cold; in* for *out; here* for *there.* Our pencil line and the blank space need one another to exist! When we forget the *act* of creation and see only the *result* of that creation, these so-called opposites, we start believing that things have independent existence, that hot can exist *without* cold or in *without* out. We even start naturally preferring one of the opposites over the other.

In the human realm, the ego is our personal, psychological agent who splits the world from its intrinsic wholeness into parts we like and want and parts we reject, and this splitting has positive and negative consequences. On the negative side, we buy into the ego's need to dominate and control, and continually pit one part of creation against another: life *against* death, time *against* eternity. Through this attitude of loving only half the world, we have no home here.

On the positive side, the ego, this fundamental desire to be, is responsible for the world of individuality and, through that lens, consciousness and self-awareness itself. It is how we get separated as foreground from the background of everything else. It is through the agency of the ego that we get to look at ourselves, to see our own reflection.

Many positive implications arise from this stance of separateness. For example, the healthy, egoic awareness that splits the world into viewer and viewed is responsible for the entire concept and existence of Beauty, a divine quality that could not come into being without the manifestation of opposites and the capacity for self-reflection. It is *we,* self-conscious, individual beings, who seek answers and reflect upon the beauty of nature. Not only does the eye of the beholder need to exist in order for there to *be* beauty, but when that eye is the eye of the healed ego, all things are beautiful.

It is because we are made of this beauty that we respond to it so deeply; true beauty always draws us deeply into our own soul and into a deep communion that not even death can touch. Our connection to beauty goes beyond the unhealthy ego's myopic vision and unites the various parts of ourselves into the Original Whole. We *can* find a home in the world because the entire created world is actually singing the same song.

When we posit an agency or being who created all of this manifestation and beauty, we call it "God" and bow our heads and open our hearts to our Creator. This reverence can happen only as the ego becomes nonreactive to opposites and learns to negotiate the difficulties encountered in the world of duality. Only then can the ego see the opposite aspects of the world and simultaneously take its place in the bigger picture of who we truly are.

SPLITS IN THE SOUL

We must remember, however, that since all of creation is made up of paired opposites, the healthy ego has its shadow as well. The unhealthy ego arises as we unconsciously, through misunderstanding and miseducation, split ourselves further and further away from the awareness of our origin until—completely split off—we believe we are unconnected, unrelated, and live a detached existence, the continuity of which is threatened on all sides by the very content of life itself. It is first threatened by other people and their needs and finally by the very existence of the opposites of life and death. It is the extremity of this separation and the trance of the ego that make us forget that on some essential level, we are truly One with all beings and all things—and I say this not on a theoretical level, but as an actual, concrete fact.

This seemingly separate existence—one of the hallmarks of the unhealed ego—causes unbearable loneliness and longing for something more connected and meaningful. This intense longing and suffering is usually dealt with in one of two ways: through spiritual search or through burying the offending reality even deeper, so that it splits further away. Of course, the attempt to feel more powerful and more in control by pushing away the offending piece of Reality ends in the individual feeling *less* powerful, *less* in control, lonelier, and bereft of genuine contact with the very wholeness of the world that he or she so deeply desires.

If we continue attempting to bury the unbearable feelings, the conflict gets more and more externalized until it leaves the realm of the self entirely, and the world and others are blamed for our plight: *"They did it to me. I would be happy if it were not for them."* It is not an exaggeration to say that wars are fought on the battlefields of Earth because we are not brave enough to fight them on the battlegrounds of our souls by consciously passing through the suffering and effort needed to unify our beings.

Both theism and nondualism attempt to address the separation, each putting forward an approach to progress that reflects its individual point of view. The heroic, dualistic path seeks to purify the ego so that any self-will is burned away, so it is filled with practices that are constructed in order to educate the ego until it sees the errors of its ways and is "pure," such as prayers, meditations, fasts, and exercises of all sorts. The nondual path (when it is distorted), on the other hand— since it sees the ego as illusory—requires only that the practitioner *stop* his or her efforts so that the luminous ground of being can shine through. Because of this, despite various practices and hints, the seeker is left to sink or swim in the great ground of being, with the (hoped for) utter trust that things are proceeding on their way in proper fashion.

So from the theistic viewpoint, *we need to get better,* and from the advaitic, *there was never a problem in the first place.* Of course, neither extreme is true. Neither the theistic nor the nondual paths are complete without the integration of the ego. From the theistic point of view, the ego cannot be truly surrendered if it is in an unhealed state. Then so-called surrender does not include the truth of the *power* of the individual self. It is only an accommodation to the difficulties of living with an unhealed ego. If the ego is not healed, the image of a perfect God is simply substituted for the problems of the smaller self. The difficulties we all have of living in a dualistic universe and having to deal with the human issues of power and powerlessness, oneness and separateness, are withdrawn from contemplation and "solved" by giving them over—like unripe fruit—to the so-called greater God. Doing this is like placing your second best apple on the altar as an offering to God. It simply is not good enough.

This "not-good-enough" is not a moral statement, but a statement of cosmic law: only to the extent that we have worked through the splits in our soul can we connect with God. Otherwise we only strengthen the false self we all needed to create in order to survive the slings and arrows of outrageous childhood. (It is possible of course, to surrender the self to God completely. But this surrender is authentic only when the self is not viewed with hatred or contempt, when its limitations are seen to spring from the very nature of the self as a simple, imperfect *bit* of creation.)

The oneness of advaitic nondualism cannot be truly achieved until the ego has been seen to be an illusion (in that it is temporary) and allowed to thrive without the violence attached to attempts to disinherit it. True non-violence is *love-in-action*. What fear is there in loving this small, separate part that thinks it is the whole? Only by loving it does it come into its own divine and nondual status: part of the One and one with the One.

FINDING OUR WAY

We need to be as precise as possible about how to approach the spiritual work of kabbalistic healing, and it might be helpful to distinguish two levels we encounter on our path. The first and most important stages of spiritual growth have to do with challenging the standard, shopworn, yet powerful ideas our ego has about the world. This is the egoic work that Western psychology does so well, and which should never be seen as separate from the spiritual path. In this way, therapy is spiritual work, and spiritual work is therapy. It is through working with our psychology that the ego is made into a proper chariot to take us further into what we call "ourselves," but which is actually the Mind and Body of God. Without this work, the ego is forever wounded and not held in love and, like any wounded part of our body, draws our attention to it and distorts the way we feel.

When the organs and other parts of the body are healthy, they function invisibly and we do not notice them, but instead see the fruits of their actions. The same is true of the healthy ego. Even this stage of the "invisible ego," however, cannot take us all the way to liberation, which is beyond concerns with the ego. Working only within the heroic or theistic model—the realm of this first stage of spiritual work—cannot bring us to the point where having or not having an ego is no longer the burning question.

To enter the second stage of spiritual work, in which the ego is brought back into the wholeness of the human being, we must have an ego that is no longer the master of the self *and* no longer the slave of God. The vividness that is necessary to make the great leap into Reality comes from the ego. It brings depth and passion to life and, with them, the means to achieve our vision. In this stage of work the ego is no longer the enemy, not because it has been vanquished—as in the heroic/theistic model—or "seen through"—as in the nondual model—but because it has become a friend. So the same sort of conflict that was necessary in the first stage is no longer relevant.

Liberation occurs when we can see simultaneously both the solidity and validity of the ego *and* its transparent, temporary nature, not aiming at one or the other state, but holding both. While in the beginning there is an "inner foe," at the next step of development there is no inner foe. Ultimate liberation, which we might call Love, knows no such boundaries and is content to let the ego exist. This contentment is what heals the ego from being the leader of an opposition sect ("me-only"), bringing it to its rightful place as the human function that sustains and directs our efforts. Then the ego is the birthplace of the individual who is divine and beautiful in his or her own right and needs no introduction to God.

When we no longer need to purify the ego out of existence, nor see it *only* as illusion and therefore deny its importance, we can surrender to choice that does *not* split the world! This type of choice can never be used to hurt another being or to fragment the world in further ways. It can never be used to do violence to the self. It is neither exclusively dual nor nondual. The more we do the work on the ego, the less of a center of gravity the ego is, and the less it can pull us out of our realization of God and Oneness.

From either direction, the theistic or nondual, this egoic work in the service of truth supports the ultimate freedom we all seek. When this level of spiritual work is done, God becomes the center of our lives, which no longer need to be defended from incursions from some imagined enemy. God is no longer an enemy. The individual self is no longer an enemy. To *be* peace and not just portray it, we need to stop our own terrorism, even against the part of us we think of as the enemy. Then we no longer need to project our pain on the outside world, but return to our Origin, which some call God. And it is the ego, our foundation in its healthy and glowing form, that is our very soul, made of Heaven even as it brings us to It.

QUESTIONS AND ANSWERS

Comment: It seems that when people are striving for the impersonal, the reality is they can't escape being personal as well. So no matter how hard they try, they are being personal when they are striving for the impersonal. That returns us to the unity.

Jason: That is true. And I am saying something even further. Even when the striving is done, when we are no longer striving for the Absolute, we still seem to be a person in this world.

Response: We can't escape that.

Jason: It would be like saying you have to be blind to see.

Question: Can you say more about how to change the ego from being an inner foe?

Jason: Some of the work we do in A Society of Souls could be described as learning to inhabit a universe. When we inhabit Briah, concepts that exist as opposites in other realms or states of consciousness can be seen to exist simultaneously, each one supporting the other. We might say that Briah is that place where the personal and the impersonal mutually arise, are dependent upon each other, and, to personify it a bit, welcome each other. When we learn to be in that state of consciousness—which we do in order to do certain types of healings—we have a new vantage point from which to understand Reality. We begin to see Reality deconstruct into its constituent parts. So concepts like *inside* and *outside* exist simultaneously as part of a larger whole; *ego* and *non-ego*, *mind* and *no mind* exist simultaneously. This gives us a large view. To do these specific healings we have to exist in that realm, which is a nondual realm where both things are accepted as equals, not as hierarchies of each other.

When we get to that state of awareness, we even begin to see the constituent parts of the ego on a psychological level. I could say, for instance, that the ego is a thought, but it is a different type of thought: in our work, we call it a "penultimate root metaphor." We find that the ego is an extremely twisted thought. I don't mean twisted in the pejorative sense, but as meaning deeply enfolded; the ego is a deeply enfolded thought. Its unfolding brings us to the realization of what the ego actually is: it is both very real and not so real at the same time. It exists and needs to be dealt with and yet has some illusory aspects as well.

The ego is kind of like an ice sculpture. If you pay someone to make an ice sculpture for a Bar Mitzvah, perhaps he will create a swan. But that creation is only temporary. On a certain level, it begins disappearing the moment it is created, very much like us, as a matter of fact! You have to pay the guy for making the swan, even though it will soon disappear. And you still have to deal with it and put all the little hors d'oeuvres and things around it. It is the same with the ego: it must be taken seriously, but not too seriously. It needs to be accepted totally as what it is, and it needs to be healed and changed so that what it really is—a kind of twist of fate—is revealed as well.

Question: I liked what you said about theism and nondualism and would love to hear you talk about that a little bit more.

Jason: Well, I can say one interesting thing about that. When you have half the picture, you have half the realization. The Buddhist Mahayana text, the Heart Sutra, puts it this way. It says, "Form is emptiness, emptiness is form." From that perspective, one would say that both theism—which is seemingly about a separate God and the distance between us and Heaven—and the nondual or the impersonal approach—which sees only Unity and does not recognize these differences—spring from the same essential core. Both are pictures, if you will, of the same thing from different perspectives.

But the Heart Sutra goes on to say, "Form is form and emptiness emptiness." This also means that the dual or deistic approach is valid just as it is: choice is part of our lives, along with everything that choice suggests, such as separateness and a centralized viewpoint from which one chooses. Here duality itself is nondual. This nondual form of choosing, which allows a thing to be itself, does not choose in reaction to, or against, or as part of a polar opposite of, something else. It makes its choice from unity.

Healing, Briah, and the Concept of Not-Making

In order to make the best use of kabbalistic healing, to arrive at the level of mastery, the healers themselves must heal. This healing, rather than being merely physical, must include the transformation of the self from a separate center of consciousness into the deeply connected state found in Briah.

THERE ARE MANY TYPES OF HEALING, including healing of the body and of the mind, the rectification of our human and planetary ecologies, political healing, and spiritual healing. Integrated Kabbalistic Healing is a new paradigm for healing that integrates a new understanding of kabbalistic wisdom, which expands upon the traditional view, along with the latest theories in quantum physics, twentieth-century psychological insight, and teachings of nonduality, into a deeply transformative healing modality.

The position of Integrated Kabbalistic Healing is that ultimately all healing—whether of the interior of the individual or of the conditions in our world—rests on the foundation of Briah, the level of understanding where we know with greater clarity than ever before the truth of the relationship between ourselves and God. I am using the word Briah not only to name a particular kabbalistic universe, but also to denote the profound sense of connection that is found in this level of consciousness. Healing involves a profound change of perspective that makes known the already-in-place relationship between God and humanity. We might say that this is the covenant the Divine makes with humanity: to always be Present.

To heal others—which from the perspective of Integrated Kabbalistic Healing is the same as healing ourselves—we have to make an evolutionary leap. Paradoxically, we need to use all our usual methods of learning to bring us to a point where we must abandon them all, even as we continue to read and learn and think in the old way. And while we spend most of our lives trying to *make* something of ourselves, to improve ourselves—whether in a career, in learning, or in wisdom— this new state exists only after all "ornamentation has been put off" (Exod. 33:5). Only *not-making* will bring us to this state. *Not-making is that condition in which things are simply what they are and we are not making "secondary somethings" out of primary experience. We engage with Reality directly.*

Stated another way, to heal fully—in the spiritual sense—we need to experience the nondual state of the acceptance of all things and all states of being, despite the ego's attempt to control Reality and choose what it likes over what it does not like. This acceptance is not just about passivity or faith that is uninformed or resigned. It is a dynamic acceptance that brings with it the possibility of engaging in the "large view" we are capable of, wherein things are simply *themselves.*

Once we learn this type of surrender, something new emerges that otherwise cannot come into being. It emerges only when we adopt the impeccable stance of allowing Reality to exist in a way that transcends our little hopes and fears.

In the world of Briah, we can truly begin to experience our egos as transparent to the activity of God, without appealing to the ego's desire to have something more profound, more secret, or more mysterious. Catering to that desire would be like feeding plates of desserts to an already addicted child: enticing, but ultimately unrewarding. Briah is a place so plain and unadorned that it is closer than the nose on our face.

It is the place that presents the ultimate challenge to our ego: the challenge to step into the unknown and see that we are stepping onto holy ground, to look and see that God is the One we are in, and not only the One in us.

APPROACHES TO HEALING

The orientation of Integrated Kabbalistic Healing can be better understood by taking a closer look at the differences between two major approaches to thinking about healing: the approach of causal intelligence and the approach of the intelligence of the heart, a phrase popularized by R. A. Schwaller de Lubicz, the Egyptologist and philosopher.

Causal intelligence is associative; it is always comparing one thing to another in order to gain understanding, always seeing the self in relationship to something else. The mechanistic result of thinking comparatively is found in the world of Assiyah as habit, and, in the world of Yetzirah, it is profoundly psychological, associative, and firmly ensconced in memory.

The intelligence of the heart is the nonassociative type of intelligence in which we are not looking for opposites. We are in that intelligence when we are not opposing doing and not-doing. Cultivating the intelligence of the heart is the briatic approach.

In the unintegrated version of Assiyah, the ego believes it is dependent upon its complete separation in order to exist. In Yetzirah, the ego is still something separate although it leans toward more connection. It can be more benign and even helpful in its role as the spiritual seeker who can point us in the right direction. It thinks, "This is how it is done. This is how I saw it done, and this is how what I am hearing compares to what I know. This is how I know who I am." At this yetziratic level, however, we still see the world through the eyes of our own separateness. By virtue of this automatic action, the world in its Wholeness is reduced to a *yesh*—that is, a "thing" or an existence—rather than a dynamic, integral, co-arising part that contains Wholeness in and of itself. The "things" in this world can be used by our comparative intelligence and lead us to a better, kinder life, but they can never bring us to Wholeness.

The heart of spiritual healing, whether formally—as in Integrated Kabbalistic Healing—or in prayer or other spiritual practices of healing and unification, appears only when we are not working within memory, when the healing takes place in the sacred arena of the Unending Moment. Causal intelligence does not produce anything original because it is always in memory, and memory cannot produce an image of our "original face," the Zen term for being connected to God, the Creator spirit, the real self. In other words, we can face God only with the face God originally gave us. Causal intelligence cannot bring true *de'vekut,* or God-cleaving. True healing requires a leap out of our history into who we are in our essence, to the Grace that exists *within us* and that makes us available to the ever-flowing Grace from above.

Although causal intelligence cannot lead us where we need to go to truly heal, it is very useful for human beings. Symbolic thinking, a form of causal intelligence, is the essential core or path of many religions, comprising the rules and regulations that make up the focus of religious practice. This approach says, "We do such-and-such an action *because* . . ." This "because" is still at the level of the symbolic, for the rule, commandment, or original creative action has not yet become a thing-in-itself.

Despite the fact that the view of the world from the perspective of both Assiyah and Yetzirah is quite limited, there is no other way to get to Briah than by going through these worlds. Working through associative intelligence is a valid approach for learning any new skill. We need to possess this kind of intelligence, for that is how we learn. We have to have it modeled for us and we have to practice it. And all of us work on that level all of the time. We might say that not only do we never give up working on that level of practice, but that the more we are committed to transcendent Reality, the more we practice being fully human. The path is: Heaven and Earth in One place. It cannot be skipped over.

Being in a so-called transcendent state (which always includes the immanence of God) can never be truly achieved as long as we are still defending ourselves from the suffering of the human condition. Going to Briah as a defense will never work. Instead, after a period of seeming peace, we will be thrust into lower worlds once more as the splits in our consciousness reemerge; we must work through what we have tried consciously or unconsciously to avoid—in this case by going to an egoic version of Briah. If we go to Briah in any way other than by working through the lower universes, we cannot live there.

EXPANDING PARADIGMS

In Briah the physical and psychological processes of Assiyah and Yetzirah come into full manifestation. While Assiyah calls for correct actions, Yetzirah deals with the emotional healing of historical hurts. Briah brings us to the unitive or nondual state, that condition which many theistic traditions have lost sight of or misinterpreted in the hard work of the first two types of healing. Briah is where we see within our separateness both the origins of our pain and the beginnings of our glory—God in Transcendence and God in Immanence.

We can talk about Briah as an exemplar or an emblem of what the unitive state looks like. It is the plainness of Truth. It is the place where opposites meet in Light. *Everything that is allowed to exist, exists in Light.* It is the place where a bush burns but is not consumed. It is the transcendent place that is completely ordinary. It is the final freedom that makes us prostrate ourselves, bringing our heads below a heart that understands. It is an experience that requires total dedication to the truth to achieve, and it is certainly not everyone's path or need. But for those whose inner force directs them to explore the depths of God's world, the type of consciousness found from the briatic perspective stands as the shimmering benchmark that beckons the spiritual traveler.

From the point of view of Yetzirah in its unintegrated state, Briah seems like a cold place. People—both ancient and modern—have spoken about Briah as a causal realm, as a place of thought and pattern. It has been visualized as a place of sacred geometry, where every line and dot is fraught with meaning. While this is true, this is only what Briah looks like from the less integrated perspective of Yetzirah. The experience of living in briatic consciousness is quite different.

Today it is easy for most of us to understand intuitively that there are things we feel and know that we keep unconscious. This notion is included in the coin of the realm of our civilization, an idea that we take for granted and spend freely. Furthermore, we now understand that many of our physical ills have psychological origins, and the study of psychosomatic medicine—the mind-body connection—is one of the forefronts of mainstream science.

But for a citizen of the early 1900s, these connections were not apparent, or were often vehemently denied. That children have active sexual imaginations was forcefully denied during Freud's lifetime in the same way that theories about plate tectonics and continental drift were denied for almost fifty years even though there was ample proof for them. In the same way, Wilhelm Reich's connection between fear of the life force, body armoring, and the lack of mental health is denied by many people today.

When we look at the new through the lens of the old, we see only what the old lens lets through, which is never the new. When we have no bodily understanding of Briah, when our understanding of Briah comes from only our thinking, Briah looks mysterious and strangely flat. We are limited only to the understanding of things that we can put into thought. It is the difference between someone who has walked the territory and someone who has only studied the map. Walking the territory changes not only our minds and hearts but our bodies as well.

But when our bodies are engaged with the level of integration that this realm actually is, the understanding of what Briah is begins to become alive and surpasses simply thinking about it. When Moses saw the burning bush, he was having an experience beyond thought or memory. He had nothing to fall back on but the immediacy of God. When Daniel emerged from the furnace, he lived in a realm beyond thought.

Briah is not a place devoid of emotions or actions or anything else, since it recapitulates all of the less integrated universes. We often speak of Briah as more essential than either Assiyah or Yetzirah. But rather than imagining Briah as the engine that makes the car run, we should think of Briah as the car itself, as the largest paradigm and not the smallest one. The entire car contains the engine, the springs, the fuel, the wheels, and, in a sense, even the roads. We could say from this perspective that cars create highways and highways create cars. The causality becomes circular instead of linear.

Thus, "the car" is the farthest-reaching paradigm, the one that affects the most things. It serves as the most integrated container for all of these important pieces that would have no function if not for the overarching context—the car—where they all find their rightful place. This is what Briah is: always the largest paradigm.

Because each of these universes—the idea of a universe being a human invention—is only a piece of the Limitless Wholeness that is the Great Luminous Silence, each universe has a limit to how much of the Totality it can hold before the very paradigms that make up that level of consciousness break and shatter.

For instance, the consciousness of Assiyah can accommodate opposites as long as they are separated in some manner: so *left* is over *there* and *right* is over *here*. Jason is *here* and not *there*. Things are separated by time and space, and we cannot be in two places at once. The sequence of "single-time-single-place" is quite important in Assiyah, which is a linear world. If someone were to show up in two places at the same time, the consciousness of Assiyah would shatter; this level of understanding cannot accommodate that piece of Reality. It would term such an event a lie, or magic, or a miracle to be given a supernatural explanation.

In Assiyah, opposites are opportunities to choose one over the other (the "right way" over the "wrong way," "good" over "bad," "our side" over "their side"). This ability to choose is the first step in any spiritual quest; we must be able to use our consciousness and will to make choices that are life affirming and life gathering. We must learn to overcome our tendencies to take roads of least resistance and run with our personal desires and instead test ourselves against what we know is right.

However, if we stay only in an assiyatic stance, we run the risk of taking on a fundamentalist and rigid point of view. We lose all appreciation for nuance and feel close only to those who think and act as we do. We believe ourselves to be "right" and others "wrong." Political problems that are solved only assiyatically ("you stay over there and I'll stay over here") are not really solved for long; they are simply put on hold.

Dictatorships—whether political or spiritual—are fundamentally assiyatic-only inventions, with the added octane of pieces of yetziratic passion, which are seen only through assiyatic eyes, eyes that cannot see the whole of Yetzirah but co-opt its ingredients to make a deadly stew.

Yetzirah, with its own strengths and limitations, is also only a piece of Reality. Opposites can be held together in Yetzirah more easily than in Assiyah. In Yetzirah, our emotional lives are often "in two different places" at the same time, such as when we love and hate the same person. When we are psychologically healthy, we can accept this simultaneous existence of opposites more easily. In the real world of Yetzirah, opposites are seen as opportunities to reconcile competing or conflicting emotions through psychological and emotional understanding.

Time is also more malleable in Yetzirah. At A Society of Souls I have seen person after person with relatively little training (which is important because a little bit of training done correctly appeals to "beginner's mind" and sets a person free of shopworn limitations and concepts) do exercises in which they are able to correctly tell another person, whom they have only recently met, specific, insightful details—whether visual, emotional, or otherwise—about that person's early life. They can do this because in Yetzirah time is bi-directional; it moves not only from past to future, but also from present to past. A skillful approach can teach us how to move in this form of time with relative freedom, something that is unthinkable or delusional from a purely assiyatic perspective.

In this way, yetziratic thinking is the great antidote to the rigidity of Assiyah. For example, after years of heartbreak and struggle, many political conflicts could be solved—and by *solved* I mean truly *revisioned*—if each of the warring factions could begin to see the other side as being composed of human beings who have needs and feelings that are not so different from their own. When we can all give to others exactly what we hope and expect for ourselves, peace begins to manifest and, with it, creativity and exchange.

The same kind of reconciliation can occur in our personal lives. We enter spiritual paths—whether therapeutic or religious—because we feel uneasy, because we suffer and desire to make peace with ourselves. Somewhere in us we have a memory of connection (which is miraculous enough!), prompting us to recognize that we do not feel the Wholeness that we somehow know should be our birthright. We give this feeling of connection many names, but we know it is a vital part of who we essentially are.

Becoming aware of these pairs of opposites—feeling we *should* be "connected" and *knowing* we are not—leads us to the spiritual quest in the hope of resolving this tension into a choice we want: to be one with God and our Real Self, to have our original face in the shimmering of the world.

SPIRITUAL QUESTING

For most of us, a spiritual quest is primarily assiyatic and yetziratic. The assiyatic spiritual quest consists of following a prescribed path, having faith that simply struggling to do the right thing will bring us into a deeper feeling of peace. It is a form of willful and bodily surrender that does not yet involve the inner person but works with the outer behavior in an attempt to reach the inner self. In a sense, the inner person has been set aside in an effort to change from being separate to belonging to something beyond oneself. This is the path of freedom through belonging.

There is a serious pitfall in remaining in this form of consciousness: namely, the accentuation of the separateness between "us" (those who follow the particulars of a prescribed path) and "them" (those who do not and who are therefore seen as not belonging to the club). However, changing one's behavior from simply reacting to outside stimuli to taking the life force in hand and making concrete changes in behavior is of vital importance and should not be underestimated.

At its best, the assiyatic-only approach allows us to pay attention to the world in a new way, to hear other people more clearly, and to behave responsibly as citizens of the world. It is a state of awareness that can foster a kind of fairness that is based not on emotional content but on a sense of fair play. It evokes the hero in all of us, someone who can put his or her body on the line for what is right.

When the spiritual path is followed courageously, it teaches us how each new level—though it brings us closer to clarity—has a particular way in which it can also *inhibit* further growth. The assiyatic danger lies in believing and acting in too rigid a manner, with too much separateness and—ironically—"clarity" between the self and other. There is, in other words, no I and Thou relationship or meeting between person and person or person and God. Yetzirah is the antidote for the rigidity of Assiyah because it is all about flow: the flow of feelings and time, the cycle of emotional life, and the unending flow of psychological and interior awareness.

Yetziratic work begins with the recognition that often pain continues despite following the outer path. We cannot stop ourselves from being hypercritical of those we love. Despite our good intentions and our following of the "way," we still feel alienated from God and other people. We feel unbearable loneliness; we are afraid of death; we are still selfish; we are anxious. We feel the need to go farther into unknown territory, and that unknown place is our own consciousness. Here we enter the world of feeling. For many of us, this is the longest part of the journey, and the most rewarding.

It is on this part of the journey that we make the deep internal connections hidden by the play of symbols in our conscious world. We find our hidden responses, our neglected memories, and come into more wholeness as connections are made between our inner, psychological life and our outer behavior. Slowly, our life changes.

There is always a danger, of course, of thinking we have found "the holy ground" and remaining on that patch of awareness far longer than it is useful to remain. The small ego reasserts itself by asking us to stop the constant process of change and connection.

When we stop our growth because our small egos are afraid to move farther along the path toward the Great Luminosity, we turn what is really a dynamic, ever-changing state into a *yesh*, a "place" or an "existence." We lose the perspective that each new level is simply a momentary stopping place, a vantage point from which we get a particular view of the unimaginable Wholeness.

At some point, Yetzirah can become an obstacle to the further integration of the Divine. Because the yetziratic view is so interested in ferreting out the meaning of each moment, of making the interior exterior through conscious understanding, it does not truly understand the profoundly dynamic state of not-making that is the hallmark of and gateway to Briah. Without the experience of not-making, the world and awareness of Briah, with its infinitely closer relationship with God, cannot be appreciated. It cannot even appear as a dynamic, living expression of God.

One of the major yetziratic pitfalls that prevent this understanding is what we might call the idea of justified pain. At some point in the spiritual journey, people come up against the deeply held belief that their pain—emotional, spiritual, or even physical—has a reason for existing, whether this be an external, an internal, or a historical reason. The reason justifies the existence of the pain.

Clearly things are not perfect in this world. We encounter imperfect conditions constantly in our present, everyday life just as we encountered them in our childhood as the children of imperfect parents. This imperfection, which is the continued inheritance of every being, causes pain.

In Assiyah, we see this pain as coming from the outside and we try to remedy it by—first of all—changing everything around us. Then, still speaking assiyatically, we try to change our own behavior to maximize our own happiness.

As our journey continues to deepen into yetziratic awareness, we can still see our pain as coming either from the outside or from psychological conditions within ourselves. We then go about trying to understand and change our own feelings so that we can be happy, whether that happiness is simply the surcease of our pain or the happiness of coming closer to God.

In either case, we believe there is some reason for our pain, and our actions are supposed to change the inner or outer conditions, through behavioral change or inner understanding, so that we can unify in some manner. At this point, our primary relationship is with a strategy, whether gross or subtle, that is supposed to bring us closer to a condition of Wholeness, which we hope will cure our pain.

At first, this work is useful and exciting. We feel we are getting somewhere—and we are! We learn the inner causes of our pain and stop blaming outer stars for the problems of our inner ones. Simultaneously, we are better able to tolerate those emotional injuries that *did* come from the "outside," the fruits of an imperfect world and imperfect people. We begin to be able to sort out our own internal suffering and the suffering that is the nature of the way the world actually is. This in turn allows us to see ourselves and the world ever more clearly. For instance, we stop feeling the need to idealize our parents and risk seeing them as limited, suffering beings who, despite their good intentions, continued their round of suffering upon us.

This work continues through many different levels. At some point, the ego becomes healthy enough—paradoxically—to see that there will never be an end to the changes necessary to end this suffering. We cannot get "pure" enough to give up resistance to loving God and others; we cannot control the world, and there are always others who treat us unfairly and who truly do not see our hearts. We see that ultimately our healing and even the healing of the world depend upon having a new relationship with ourselves at every moment.

It is at that moment that we begin to suspect that something new must be brought to bear, that we need some new tool to help us on this part of the journey. We begin to see that if something is not done, the very work of finding meaning and purification will become an obstacle in and of itself because of the impossibility of eradicating this omnipresent imperfection.

This truth of imperfection teaches us that we cannot simply alternate between universes in an effort to escape imperfection. Instead, we need to *integrate* them—that is, integrate assiyatic action with yetziratic feeling with the transcendent knowing of Briah. In this way we achieve freedom.

The gatekeepers of Briah are these: when you have done enough historical work—that is, when you have sincerely stopped looking outside yourself for the source of any of the real difficulties in life—then briatic work begins. When you have stopped looking outside yourself for salvation, briatic work begins. Only when you have entered into yourself can you receive the most effective help. This does not mean that yetziratic work like psychotherapy or working with practices or traditions stops. It simply means that a shift has taken place and we see that the problems and the difficulties we face, as well as the solutions and the resources we have to overcome them, are all within us. We bring our feelings, our problems, and all our daily life to a new level of consciousness, which we can call briatic.

Our commitment to this level of integration means that, more firmly than ever, we go through our life riding the wave of resistances to God's world and word, taking everything that happens into ourselves. This doesn't mean that we do not continue to try to change our consciousness and personality. It does not mean that we abandon the path of purifying ourselves and our physical, emotional, and spiritual environment. It means we are looking, all the time, to be as impeccable as possible about noticing the world as it is, so that we can be in its Mystery. Our most profound tool in this quest is nonreactive grace, allowing things to be simply what they are, which is what I have referred to as "not-making."

NOT-MAKING

Making something is the realm of Yetzirah and Assiyah. Briah is the realm of not-making. All opposites are held together in Briah, however, so while things are still made in Briah, they are *made* by the action of *not-making.* I call this "God-making." This is entirely different from human-making, which is making from memory, making the same thing over and over again. God-making is making something from nothing. It occurs when we are in touch with our God-given originality.

Entering into Briah, far from being some steady-state you achieve once and for all, needs to be invented afresh every time you do it. This means you never get expert at it, but rather—through a kind of beginner's mind—you must face the ego and its demands every time you think you want to be with God. Each time you pray or sing or heal or help, you have to ride the wave of these difficulties—which is another way of saying that you have to live with your terror of the unknown— to enter a place where everything is important and where relationship is the primary governing metaphor.

Briah is also that place where each member of an opposite pair takes on a new role and possibility. When freed from its identity as part of a polar pair, and seen as a thing-in-itself, it can lead us to increasing levels of Wholeness as we let it exist and express its True Nature. This process of seeing each thing as a thing-in-itself brings us into the Now.

Healing exists because there is a Now that we can enter. We do not encounter this Now until we are willing to give up memory—which does not mean forgetting, but actually means *remembering,* remembering enough so that we are free of it. For example, we know what words to use to describe the setting sun, but the experience of the sun setting is always fresh, and we can be touched by its beauty in a way that does not let us speak falsely.

Imagine you are with a friend and the sun goes down. You are talking and you haven't even been watching the sunset. Suddenly the sky becomes ablaze with beauty, and you say, "Oh! Wow! Look at that!" And the wonder is inside you and outside you at the same time, even if you found a beautiful way to say it, or even if you said to your friend, "Oh my God, look at that. It makes me feel sad. Another day, the earth is turning away from the sun. Another day never to be recaptured. I want to run after the sun and keep it on the horizon forever." It doesn't matter what you say. It is irrelevant whether the event makes you feel happy or sad or mortal or immortal. There is something about that event that, if you let it in, makes you totally fresh when you relate to it. It is not owned by you; rather *you* are owned by *it*. And yet, paradoxically again, you are *you* and it is *it*. You know the difference and the impenetrable gulf between the poles of this experience. There is both discriminating awareness and Oneness.

This is true healing, the healing we might call the presence of God. It is the Pure Present. It is not in memory. When we are not in reactivity, we have the possibility of being in nonreactive grace. We have the possibility of feeling the ever-flowing Grace that the All-Loving One bequeaths upon all existence. We can then feel lighthearted.

This is the stage of work where no one can do anything to you anymore and no one can save you. You save yourself. It is you who has to walk to God. God has already walked to you. God is here. The Shema tells us that God cannot *not* be here; therefore it is we who need to get unwound and uncontracted enough so that we do not believe that there is distance. Then we are in Briah, our small self still existent but now in Light.

CONTRACTING AND EXPANDING

Until we are healed, the flow of what is happening right now—which is always the play of the Divine, the communication that God is making with us—is extremely challenging for us to bear as separate individuals. Paradoxically, our so-called psychological problems are one way we take ourselves out of this flowing dynamic Wholeness to a place we believe is safe—or at least less threatening to our small selves.

From one perspective, these problems are like little homesteads that we make for ourselves, usually populated with bad characters. These psychological problems are contracted states. They are contracted against the pulsating movement of Life. That is really all they are from the perspective of Briah.

These contracted states then take on a life of their own. They have consciousness because we are enclosing a piece of the creative plenum, and they begin to look at themselves. These contracted states make us think that there is something in the world called "people," at the expense of processes, relationships, and interactions. These "people" then think they have territory to defend and a position to defend. That is neurosis, and it is passed down from generation to generation.

At a certain point—and this is the moment that the door to Yetzirah opens—we say to ourselves: "I need to find out what is true. *Why* am I reactive? *What* am I reacting to? I need to know." This movement is the movement from Assiyah to Yetzirah, from habit to feeling, and it brings with it a loss of clarity that comes from leaving the comfortable world of black-and-white distinctions.

Entering into the exploration of the psychological world, we do not know if something that is bothering us actually *is* inside our own reactivity or is something on the outside that needs to be changed or addressed. We spend our time in this "middle stage" of the spiritual journey, separating the wheat from the chaff, finding out who we are. Despite the fact that we are now dealing directly with feelings, this is a rationally oriented part of the journey, and it is because of this rational bias that we get confused.

To paraphrase an old Zen saying: In the beginning of Zen there are mountains and rivers. During Zen there are no mountains and no rivers. After Zen there are mountains and rivers. In other words, we start out knowing how to apportion the world and work with the world, then we make some sort of transition. Everything goes *kablooie*. Here is the river; here is the mountain. But the mountain has some riverness to it and the river has some mountainness to it, and they both flow and they both meet each other. One makes the other. As the great Zen master Dogon-zenji used to say, "The mountains are walking."

Eventually things return to themselves, but in order for that to happen, the next stage of spiritual development—which involves the world of Briah and the condition of not-making—must come to the fore. The world must be taken whole. At this moment of transformation, this point of reorientation, a new paradigm comes into being. This new attitude says, in effect: "Whether this suffering is caused by something that is still within my own psyche or by outer circumstances, I need to feel it and experience it exactly as it is. I need to stop trying to save myself from it or the pain it causes me. Neither do I need to embrace it as some sort of penance or teacher. I need to be present and do nothing to or with it. I need to stop making, and allow the dynamic intelligence of the situation, which sits right below the surface of appearances, to manifest, and along with it, the Light of God."

Let me illustrate this with a story. A few years ago, as I was leaving Lexington, Massachusetts, after visiting some friends, I stopped at a bagel shop for breakfast. I had been in a sort of state of grace for the two days of my visit. I was still feeling that way that morning, at least until I entered the bagel shop. I got in line to order my sandwich and immediately saw that the shop was severely understaffed. There was one teenager at the grill, one at the counter taking orders, and one at the cash register, with a line of twenty people, ready to have breakfast, snaking out the door onto the street.

So, even though I didn't think I was feeling particularly urgent about having breakfast, after about ten minutes in line I said to the fellow standing next to me, "Well, they're not really set up for volume here, are they?" He replied, "If you want McDonald's, you should have gone to McDonald's."

Now, as I mentioned, I had been in a state of grace. Because of this exalted state, and the years of training I had, and my impeccable briatic consciousness, I was able to have enough presence of mind to get past my desire to throttle him. After I got past my desire to attack him or ignore him, I finally said, "Do *you* want to go to McDonald's?" which was the best I could come up with in the moment.

He said, "No. That's why I'm standing here." And I said, "Me too," and we continued waiting in silence.

So I had become reactive. Why? Because he—I imagined—humiliated me. Because of my childhood history of being criticized, I interpreted this fellow as saying that I was less than something: less than him, or less than a good person should be, or something like that.

The truth is, even if this fellow *was* saying something like that, he was someone I would never, ever see again and someone who, as a stranger, did not know my heart. Yet it was somehow important enough for me to tighten my chest and legs and attempt to give him a sassy comeback. I had fallen, right there in the bagel shop, out of grace and into my history.

But until that moment of understanding, I believed that there was still some justification for my displeasure with him. In other words, the one in me who felt he still had to defend his ground from the slings and arrows of past, *real* humiliation still existed. It was this piece of my history that was calling the shots. Since this part of me was mostly unconscious, operating behind the scenes, I consciously believed this fellow was disrespecting me. I also believed that this disrespect could harm my essential nature.

We are rational creatures and we think that we have a right to our feelings because "this situation was like this, and this was like that, and so on and so on." In these circumstances we feel morally justified. *I* felt morally justified in this case.

There I was in the bagel shop, waiting for breakfast, flowing. I was noticing everything: the young fellow behind the counter making sandwiches, my wife sitting down at the table . . . and then I made a comment to the fellow next me. The guy made a comment back: "You want McDonald's, you should go to McDonald's." And I contracted out of the flow, thinking, "There is a *he* who just attacked a *me* and that *me* has to defend *me*," and I was no longer in the state of grace, in God's space. Really, at that moment, I wanted to simply make contact, but I didn't know how to do it, so I substituted something that was not quite true, and the rest—and the beginning—is history.

It is true that that moment activated a wound perpetrated upon me when I was seven, but continuing the existence of the wound is something I have to do actively in the moment. And if I haven't dealt with my wound since I was seven, then this wound has had a life of its own all that time, living in there, happily spinning around in its own little circle thinking that it is a thing with no connection to what is flowing outside in the world. It simply sits there, waiting to react.

If I did not have that place in me that could be humiliated, or if I had been able to feel that vulnerable place in me without shattering— that is, without "going unconscious" or defending against it or acting it out (another way of not feeling its impact)—I could have seen him, myself, and the entire structure with great clarity. I would have ridden the wave of transference. I would have been in *nonreactive* grace. As it was, I felt humiliated because of his perceived critical comment. I in turn humiliated him, and we then both spent the remainder of our short relationship making up with each other by signs and body language and short moments of connection.

Nonreactive grace doesn't mean: "I can take it. The world can do whatever it wants to me. It won't affect me." That is not nonreactive grace. Rather, it occurs when you have worked through the trouble in yourself and you can accept what is in you. It occurs when you know what the trouble is, and when you have real and deep forgiveness for yourself as well as the people who made you the way you are. And whether the problem is completely gone or you simply have exquisite awareness of it, either is all right. Then you are in Briah. In Briah all of the human things happen. You learn about yourself. You learn about other people. You see the difficulty of being human. You have compassion. You can take care of yourself if you need to take care of yourself. You are free, not a slave to your precious, personal feelings.

I read in a Buddhist magazine of someone's idea that Buddhahood was when a person had no sexual feelings, no anger, didn't get upset about anything, and had no "evil thoughts." To me, this is a kind of Hollywood Zen. We could call it dead Zen. It is not that there is no anger and there is no ability to defend in the realized state of briatic consciousness. But when we defend ourselves from a self-realized place, we are defending life itself and not the temporary egoic situation to which life has attached itself. When a mother defends her baby, she is doing something more than personal at that moment. She is defending life itself. This is being with God.

But when we defend ourselves from a contracted state, we create separation. When we believe that we are only that *thing* our contraction tells us we are, that is what we see in other people and in the universe: other things. Then we can relate only to other things. Then we meet somebody and our thing relates only to his or her thing. If it is sexual, we know what the things in question are. It is not the whole person. If the thing we relate to is our neurosis, we see his or her neuroses. Then our life is only a story of how we relate to different things. We find ourselves in our own movie: "Well, first I did this and then this happened to me." This is a stage of work we need to do and we need to continue doing. It goes on simultaneously with the holy work of Briah.

But there is another level of work where story-making is no longer so interesting. Maybe this is why gossip is a sin in most religions, because it makes us think that the story is important. It takes us out of the flow of life. "Did you see what Harry did? My God!" Harry is this thing, and Harry does this thing to these other things, and therefore Harry is a bad thing. And on it goes.

When we are involved in this world of thingness instead of anything else, we are closed off. Then in this world of thingness, generosity of spirit goes out the window because generosity is not a thing. I am not talking about sentimentality. That is a thing. I am not talking about altruism. That is a thing too: "I should be good. I should think of those less fortunate than myself. I should sacrifice something of my own self so that someone else can have." This way of relating to the world reeks of thingness. What I am talking about is true generosity, which happens when you give something away before you know you have it. Or it may be simpler than that; it may be just generosity of spirit, allowing the other guy to exist even if he is different. That orientation goes out the window when we think we are a thing. Urgency climbs in the window instead. Only someone who is not a thing can give something of lasting value.

In Briah, the personal and the transcendent are both present. It is not a place where we say, "Well, we have transcended the personality. We are past the personality. We are in Briah." No. Briah is the interface between personality and the transcendent. They are both present. It is even the place from which we know we will go on making stories, being imperfect, failing and falling because we are human.

Yetzirah without Briah is pure personality and history. There is no transcendent function. There is no overview. Briah without Yetzirah is powerful and useful, but austere, cool, conceptual, and without kindness and true forgiveness.

True Briah comes when the transcendent vision is extended to the personality. When this extension occurs, we have something transcendently warm and generous. We accept each thing as a thing-in-itself, and therefore move out of comparative intelligence and into the wisdom of the heart.

When we have done that, when we have extended Briah's transcendent vision to the personality, we then can have warmth and generosity and accept each thing in its own self. And just by that type of acceptance, we return each thing to its original nature. Then to us, living in that felicitous milieu, the highest and the lowest, the mundane and the transcendent, Heaven and Hell, do not concern us because we know we are always with God. We do not care where we are on the continuum between so-called highest and so-called lowest because higher and lower are seen as the same thing. They are not our concern. We are content at that point to let God guide us through the Mystery of life. That is real surrender.

One of the Sufi names for God is the "One Who Returns." This means that being with God returns us to the time before we named the world. That is what humans do. That is what happens in Genesis: Adam names. We are all Adam. When we name the world, we are making it into *something*. This is very useful and we need to be able to do it. Science is built on that. It is very useful, for example, to know that the bacillus on a certain plant is the same bacillus that causes an ailment in humans but somehow plants don't get ill from it. Then we are prompted to ask whether there is something in the plant that inhibits the reproduction of this germ and whether we can develop an antidote for human beings from what we learned. It is useful to name the world, to identify and fix it.

But for our purposes as spiritual warriors, as people who want to walk "the Way," as people who want to surrender to the Great What Is, only naming the world makes it into something, and that limits who we truly are and who we understand God to be. Returning to God by not naming, but being awake, we return to our Essence. It is a return to the Place before naming. When we have practiced this form of return long enough, we can return to the world and begin to name the world without limiting it. We can live in the world as free beings who can worship the Creator. We feel it in our bones. We realize that good and bad thoughts are just thoughts. Happy and sad feelings are just emotions. And the body is simply the temporary home of something that travels through life and death like a wave. *We are here, we are not, we are here, we are not,* and what we really are continues. We have a new perspective.

If we want to go all the way back to the Ayn-Sof, the Nameless, Endless One, God brings us to the place before we named the world. And then the strange and wonderful thing happens. We find that we turn over our free will to God and name the world all the names God has already named it. We could call ourselves then the "one who names." We worship because there is nothing else to do when confronted by the clear sight of What Is. We continue learning; we continue along with our human failings, but not identified with them, free to thank God for giving them to us since the gift of our suffering is also the gift of our healing.

And we heal our small world and the results emanate, like the sounds of a blessing spoken almost silently at night.

QUESTIONS AND ANSWERS

Question: What did you learn from the encounter in the bagel shop?

Jason: I learned about myself, and I was pointed toward freedom. He was a teacher to me. My feeling of humiliation, which stemmed from a memory of somebody criticizing me in my childhood, made the world and was continuing to make the world. Once I saw that and accepted it totally, I was free not to act on my impulse of self-preservation. Then I could see that he and I were not antagonists, on opposite sides of a battle to stay afloat or sink in childhood pain. We were two beings with a common bond, two beings having breakfast, ordering reality sandwiches. That doesn't mean we were entirely free of our histories. Simply holding my history in its entirety without defending against it freed me to see we were two imperfect souls in a bagel shop.

My feeling of humiliation originated from a fossilized thought. Thought—believed to be Reality itself—can only separate us from the world. Thought is the eddy in the water, the wavelets that happen when the water is disturbed. It is a wonderful thing. It reflects the light. It refracts the light. It makes the ocean interesting. It is a form of creativity. But thought separates us from knowledge of the Whole if we think we are the thought and the thought only. If we are not identified with some state of being, some *yesh,* we are free. We have thought and no-thought, and we are free to be as human as we want. And that level of integration is where we are connected to God and able do God's will because it is our own deepest desire.

In Briah, *thinking* still operates but *thought* does not. When you are deeply engrossed in conversation with somebody, and the two of you are working out a problem, saying, "Why don't we look at this problem in this way?" you are in Briah. Who is talking and who is listening at that point? Do you have consciousness of that? You do not. You are not saying, "Well, here is my thought about this." You are not reflecting on thought, or having thoughts about thinking; rather, you are thinking itself, completely in the present moment.

When you are deeply involved in dialogue, there is no subject or object, there is no higher or lower. Whatever you are working on is the important central thing. That feeling is briatic. The ego exists in Briah. We still answer to our name. From the briatic point of view, the ego can direct us and inform us, but it does not rule us.

Question: Could you explain the distinction you made between thought and thinking in some other way?

Jason: Let's look at what occurred just now. First, you were thinking of asking me a question and you were in a sort of dialogue with yourself, holding the question in memory as you got ready to speak. Then, as you spoke the question, you disappeared: there was no self-reflection for a moment. A thought form is a piece of paralyzed past, but at that moment of speaking, you were free to be in the present.

In Briah our suffering is our own. Everybody in this room is suffering to one extent or another.

Try this for a moment: Just close your eyes and think to yourself, "This suffering is truly my own." Put it back in your body. It is like a knapsack that you are going to walk around with. That is all it is, a backpack. It is not the end of the world. It is your history, which you can keep with you and be free of at the same time. What happens when you do that? Are there any changes in your consciousness or your physical feeling?

Audience member: It's a relief, relaxation, peace. I feel increased vulnerability, acceptance, and more whole.

Jason: Isn't this simple? What we are talking about now are the doorways into Briah. Briah is an infinite realm. There are going to be lots of other experiences in Briah. But the doorway into Briah begins here, simply in taking back our suffering from any place it might be and just sweeping it back into our own hearts. I do that sometimes. I just sweep back all the little tendrils I put out thinking that other people control my life. I sweep them back until suddenly after I sweep back the last one, something entirely different happens. I begin to feel connected to something more important than my suffering, something I could notice only if all the tendrils I put out to escape my suffering were pulled back.

Audience member: It is like sweeping back your attachments.

Jason: Yes. This is a very important statement. It is important because there are many paths that talk about nonattachment. If you try to approach nonattachment prematurely, what does it look like? It looks like dissociation and detachment. We cannot do what we are not truly ready for. It would not be prudent, for instance, to suggest that somebody do briatic work when that person is doing the hard work of trying to recover a healthy ego from his or her history. We don't want to talk about "transcending the ego." It is self-secret in that we understand it only when we are ready. Suggesting transcendence before a person is ready is certainly not using skillful means or kindness or compassion.

Audience member: When I took in my suffering and accepted it, it felt like it became very spacious and then drifted away. Then I understood that the suffering was a passing thing but that I usually attach to it and suck it in; I create my own suffering that way.

Jason: Yes. Beautiful. Let's take an example of one type of psychological work, the type that works with characterologies. Characterologies are egoic in the sense that they define and pin down reality to an "already-thought" thought. We could call them *thunks*. Are they useful? Yes, and they have vitality because originally they were somebody's thinking. The ego loves everything that has already been thought. It can use these thoughts as a tool, over and over again, as a hedge against the danger that it will fall into its great fear: the Unknown. Characterologies can be very helpful, but they do not have that spark of life in them that we are looking for if we are trying to get to God. In fact, they call for memorization and they go into memory, and it is memory that is the maker of things and the killer of the Present Moment.

Question: So where does humor come in?

Jason: Right now. I'm not feeling threatened now. If I hadn't been feeling threatened in the bagel shop, I could have just as easily have said, "Yeah, compared to this place McDonald's is like the Holy Grail." I could have said anything. I could have said the right funny thing that would have made him laugh and made me laugh. I could also have said nothing.

F O U R

The Healing of Immanence and the Nature of God

Man does many things to achieve one thing; God does One thing to achieve many things.

—G. T. FECHNER, 1835

THE HEALING OF IMMANENCE—the first of the many kabbalistic healings taught in the Integrated Kabbalistic Healing training of A Society of Souls—is profoundly simple: it only asks us to acknowledge that there is no place devoid of God and, as healers, to receive the already-in-place-Divinity of our client. This is the opposite of many types of healing modalities, in which we bring something *to* the client. Here, we receive.

This is so because the clearer we get and the more work we do on ourselves, the more we see what Reality truly is. We see the laws of the universe at work. The more we understand ourselves, the more we understand others and the universe in which we live.

We begin to see that every bit of earth, air, mind, and feeling has within it all of the universe; that God is expressed in each and every jot; and by simply being aware of this, we can ride this powerful truth farther into the unknown, which is the Mystery of God.

Well over one thousand people now know the Healing of Immanence. It has been used—when indicated by our diagnostic process—at the birth of babies and the passing of souls. I have taught this healing in public workshops because it is extremely safe to do and easy to explain. Yet in profound private discussions among experienced kabbalistic healers, we have all marveled at the fact that the power and efficacy of this healing seems endless. No matter how many new things we understand about ourselves and the world and what Spirit asks of us, the Healing of Immanence is there, ready to take us farther. No matter how much we are able to surrender to the shimmering Name, the Healing of Immanence asks us to go a little deeper. No matter how many times we have been awed by how this healing has helped people who are suffering, we have repeatedly been humbled to learn that it can do even more.

THREE WAYS OF LOOKING AT THE WORLD

The import of the Healing of Immanence, its true scope and purview, can be better comprehended with the aid of three major paradigms or different ways of looking at the world: the holographic paradigm, the fractal paradigm, and the idea of the strange attractor.

Holographic Paradigm

A transmission hologram—that is, a three-dimensional picture that reveals different three-dimensional features as you move around it—is created by a different process than that used to make a photographic negative. No lens is used. The holographic negative is made with two laser beams, one acting as a reference beam and the other traveling a more direct path to illuminate the object. Both beams fall on the negative film. When coherent light is retransmitted through the negative, one sees, reconstructed in space, the original three-dimensional object.

Ordinary photographic negatives contain pictorial information in a recognizable format. A picture of a house will look like a picture of a house, though it will appear with dark and light tones reversed. If I take a picture of you standing next to a house, and then cut off that side of the photograph, when the photo is printed, you will be missing from the scene. You are on the cutting-room floor. So we could say that in an ordinary negative, all information is local: information that is in one area of the entire negative is only in that area.

The properties of a holographic negative are different and somewhat remarkable. A transmission holographic negative does not look like the object that has been photographed. It looks like a series of squiggles and lines because it is actually the pattern made by the interference between the two laser beams. This interference, or moiré pattern, gives information not only about light intensity but also about the relationship between the two beams of light that illuminated the object.

When coherent light is put back through a holographic negative, it resolves into a three-dimensional image. But because the negative has squiggles and lines, it stores the information in a nonlocal way, giving it some very unusual properties.

For one thing, if I took a holographic picture of you standing next to a house (which would have to be done in such a way that all noncoherent light was eliminated, such as in a studio), then cut off a corner of the negative and passed coherent light through it again, I would still see the whole picture, but a little bit less clearly. In fact, if I threw away three quarters of the negative and only used a quarter of it, I could still see the whole picture, only less clearly and with the three-dimensional effect diminished somewhat. Theoretically, this phenomenon would be true no matter how small the section of the negative was, conditioned only by how much information was in the original holographic negative. The information that is the image of the person in front of the house is in some way spread out through the entire negative, in the pattern of relationships between the wave forms of light.

The holographic negative thus represents a different paradigm. Instead of the paradigm of locality—that is, "*Here* is different from *there*," or "*This* part of the negative is the part that is the house and *that* part of the negative is the person"—we have a paradigm that says "Everything in this picture, house, sky, person, is intertwined in such a way that every bit of the negative contains the entire set of information in the originally formed negative, albeit smaller and with less clarity."

When you put light through even a particle of that hologram, you get the whole picture. This has remarkable philosophical implications. We can think of every particle or piece as being a portal to the whole. The holographic nature of things could be called a *horizontal* function: the whole universe is contained in every piece.

Fractal Paradigm

A second, equally important, concept is derived from something called fractal geometry. A mathematician named Benoit Mandelbrot, continuing the work of Edward Lorenz and others, discovered that one can create a series of points by iterating or computing a rather simple formula over and over again. Because of the nature of the formula, the data change ever so slightly each time it is computed. When the mathematical points that result from computing this formula are plotted, shapes that appear organic result. While the earliest experiments formed very simple organic forms, later versions made by Mandelbrot—using seemingly random data, like the changing price of cotton or the depth of flooding of the Nile River—came out looking like mountain ranges and other natural phenomena when they were plotted as mathematical diagrams.

But this was only part of the story. Mathematicians soon realized that if one looked at any piece of the entire shape, at any level of scale or magnification, the original shapes were essentially repeated at that new level, over and over again.

Let's say that the big shape is like a squiggly line. If a little section of that line is magnified, it will not resolve itself into a new shape—such as a straight line—but will look very much like the original squiggly line. If that level is magnified again, the same thing will happen. These fractal shapes, then, have self-similarity on all levels of scale. It is like peering into ever-smaller pieces of infinity.

This is the principle of self-similarity: the universe—from the spiral of galaxies to the spiral of DNA, from the kidney's branchlike structures to the folds in the brain—seems to be constructed in such a way that there is a connecting link between many levels of reality. It is almost as if all of reality were trying to express some similar, fundamental idea through many levels of creation. We might call this the *vertical* function.

Strange Attractor

The last and perhaps most important paradigm to consider is the idea of *strange attractors.*

Let me tell you a story of how mathematicians *might* have found the first strange attractor. If you plot the pulse of a heartbeat over a period of time, you will see that a heartbeat is vastly different from the ticking of a clock. A heartbeat is not regular. It has a certain rhythm, but it is not metronomically regular. If you plot the periodicity of the beats—that is, the time between beats—you will notice that all the points seem to cluster around a central area in which there are no or very few beats. The graph reveals a central emptiness, as it were. It is as if the idea of *beating*—and of life itself—can be expressed only indirectly, irregularly. It is as if there is some central idea present and all of the points array themselves around this central hub.

From this point of view, a heartbeat is a nonregular, nonrandom system. Mathematically and philosophically speaking, it has many of the qualities of a chaotic system. While there is a certain level of chaos in the healthy heartbeat, it is a special type of chaos, within which lies a hidden, new level of order, enfolded and implicate, subtle but pervasive. When the heartbeat gets *too* chaotic—when it loses its relationship to this invisible center—a person's heart has gone into fibrillation, a dangerous and often fatal type of chaos. Very, very small changes in any of the values of this essentially nonlinear system affect the whole system dramatically. It is as if the entire structure, endlessly moving and dynamic, were balanced on the head of an invisible pin.

This central emptiness was originally called a *Lorenz attractor,* after the mathematician who first found it by looking at data he was using to try to understand such things as weather patterns, the flow of water, and the movement of certain machines. Once alerted to this underlying order in chaos, scientists started finding that this condition was true of all natural systems, not only weather systems, but entire ecosystems as well.

Recently, using the orbiting Hubble Telescope, scientists have found areas in the universe where there are billions of galaxies that seem to congregate around a big empty space. This notion of a galactic strange attractor (to physicalize this mathematically dynamic idea) is attracting much attention.

What is a strange attractor? This rich territory is still being explored. But one thing that we have begun to understand is that certain extremely simple laws or formulae can be used to get an infinite number of variations. These variations represent a new type of orderly or deterministic chaos and have features that extend from the very big to the very small, tying together the micro and the macro in a form of union.

Kabbalistically speaking, this would mean that when God was creating the universe, He didn't have to say, "I am going to write down what everything is going to look like," thereby filling each particle of the universe with an infinite amount of linear information. God would have to say only, "Here is the law. Here is the strange attractor, and out of this the world will unfold in all of its infinite difference." God would notice the wing beat of each sparrow because God would be each sparrow as well as everything else. God's action would be holographic, and affect all levels of creation at once, and therefore become the basis of Reality's self-similar nature. We would be made in God's image, a tiny, true piece of the Divine Whole.

Here is an example suggested to me by the chaos thinker Michael Bratnick. There is a strange attractor we might call "oak tree." We all know what an oak tree is: a tree with a certain type of bark and leaves. But within the strange attractor of "oak tree," the *idea* of "oak tree," how many variations are there? An infinite number. Not only are there different types of oak trees, but no oak leaf is exactly like any other oak leaf. In fact, we might say that each leaf is unique on every oak tree in the world. And yet they are all oak trees because they are all within the *phase space* defined by this strange attractor called an oak tree. All oak trees, in other words, are expressing the unmanifested central idea of "oak tree."

The central idea can also be seen as a simple law: the existence of an infinite number of oak trees in the physical world, from Brooklyn to Tokyo, can be explained by a small string of genetic code, a finite series of protein pairs that link in a particular sequence. From this finite number of pairs of amino acids, which are found in every oak tree, we get an infinite number of leaves that are different. The result is the *infinite unlimited* and the *limited particular* holding hands. This is the True Oneness of God in the marriage of the Absolute and the relative.

TREE OF LIFE

The marriage of the Absolute and the relative is depicted in the diagram known as the Etz Chaim, or Tree of Life. The Etz Chaim—which reached its present form around 250 years ago—is a two-dimensional representation of how God's Attributes are distributed in the created world.

These Attributes, or *sephirot,* are distributed among male and female, passive and active, "strengths," and "loves." We might call them the *quanta* of the universe, the *strings*—to borrow a term from physics—upon which the existence, appearance, and workings of our universe depend. Like *strings*, these Attributes would also not be only "celestial" or spiritual. They would not be separate from us in any way. We—our bodies, minds and spirits, our very consciousness and self-awareness—would be built of these same components we are calling sephirot, as depicted in an array we call the Tree of Life.

From this perspective, God is identical with these Attributes while the sum of these Attributes is *not* identical with God! In this way, the sephirot—pictures in a fractally potent, holographic, and linear diagram, with paths and associations aplenty—become gateways to our return to the state of union we are actively *made from,* but of which we have lost awareness. (Please see the glossary for more detailed information about each of the sephirot.)

When we look at the Tree of Life diagram in light of the three paradigms—holographic, fractal, and strange attractor—we see that it is both self-similar and holographic. As shown in the diagram on page 80, each *sephira* (the singular of sephirot) has within it an entire Tree of Life.

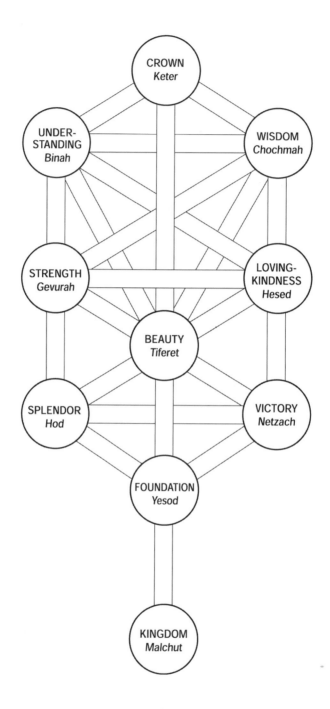

Figure 4.1. The Tree of Life

And, of course, each of those inner sephirot has within it yet another complete Tree—and so on and so on to infinity. This makes the Tree self-similar on every level. It is also holographic; as a result of the infinite levels of self-similarity, *all* the Attributes are found in each "instance" of existence. So the Attribute of *Yesod,* for instance—which has to do with the foundational drive of life for union, among other things—is found not only in the sephira that bears its name, but also in every other sephira, within the theme and consciousness each one of them *is* and represents.

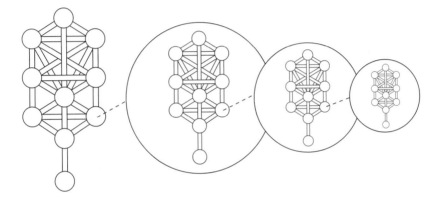

Figure 4.2. Trees within trees

To see the strange attractor aspect of the Tree of Life, we need to step back and ask where God appears in the Etz Chaim, given that the sephirot are Attributes of God and not God's Self. When we look carefully—and by *looking* I mean feeling, embodying, and knowing with the heart—we see that God is not shown in this diagram, but is the raison d'être of its existence. In other words, the Tree of Life is the evidence of something that is too far beyond conception to describe or name, but which is responsible nonetheless for all of creation, including the Attributes that are pictured in this noble diagram.

None of the sephirot is God, but God stands in the middle, making all this expression possible. Who is the One whose Attributes are Crown, Wisdom, Understanding, Loving-kindness, Strength, and Beauty?

God-ing is the face behind all expression, and all of God's laws are laws that exist in the manifest universe in a holographic and self-similar manner. This is the Real.

ORIGINS OF THE HEALING OF IMMANENCE

The Healing of Immanence developed as one of the first applications of my understanding of Kabbalah and healing. It is actually the outgrowth of the recognition of an infinite law: *The Divine is everywhere. God is everywhere. There is no place without God.* It is one of the fundamental truths of this universe and it is the message, loosely translated, of the Shema: "Hear, O Israel, the Lord our God is Singular, One and not two." A mathematician might put this truth one way, a logician some other way, a biologist yet another way, and a theologian still another way. As a kabbalistic healer concerned primarily with the healing of the human body, mind, and spirit, I am most interested in applying this law to people and the world around us.

The Tree of Life—by its very organization and pattern—shows us yet another holographic truth: God's Attributes, and by implication God's Self, have something to do with *relationship*. Without precise and yet infinitely flexible relationships, the Tree of Life as a depiction of existence cannot endure at all.

When this law of God's omnipresence and relational nature is applied to the healing of another person, we begin to see certain things immediately. The first thing it tells us is that Wholeness has something to do with relationship, and that this Wholeness is beyond separation or contradiction and holds within it the secret of what healing is.

The Tree of Life tells us that relationship is one of the root characteristics of this universe, and that we are conceived in the image of the great transparency that is God—which is to say, *fully in relationship*. If God is One, by definition no division is permissible. Therefore, one of the first ramifications of this primary Oneness is that it forms the basis of relationship itself. This Oneness is the connecting link among all things, despite the seeming difference in appearance, place, time, or outlook. This is Oneness that does not even nullify duality. It sees within duality itself—just as it is—only union.

My insight into the connection between these universal laws and the practice of healing is what led to the creation of the Healing of Immanence. While developing Integrated Kabbalistic Healing, during a period of some months, I kept the Shema in my mind and body at all times. I tried to put up everything I did against this wonderful teacher to see what the truth was.

One day, a woman came into my healing room with a problem in her quadriceps muscle. I placed my hands on her, ready to "send" energy into her in order to facilitate healing. As I touched her, the Shema went through my head: "Hear, O Israel, the Lord our God, the Lord is One." Suddenly I thought, "Where am I taking God from and bringing God to?" In other words, if this pray-statement called the Shema was true, then God was already present in this woman's leg. Why then did I need to bring God from someplace else? This was a revelation to me.

All of my training as a healer up until that point had taught me to do something, or to give something. Now I knew that to heal her, I simply had to receive the already present Divinity within her.

That meant that healing would consist of getting out of the way, so that I could receive this Divinity. But my thoughts and concepts and doubts, all of which desperately wanted me to do something to earn my keep, so to speak, intruded. My logical mind rebelled: how could receiving her Divinity actually heal her? And, the longer I did the healing, the better *I* felt! Was this okay? Shouldn't she be the one who was healed and I the one who was tired from giving?

"Getting out of the way" did not mean simply allowing or going into an oceanic state, transcending all my separated thoughts, nullifying them in trance. On the contrary, these thoughts had to be fully recognized for what they were *before* they could be put aside. And because the true nature of Oneness included even the separations of duality such as thoughts, *nothing needed to be done,* except the conscious awareness and recognition of these facts.

Let us reexamine what was really happening in the light of what we have talked about so far. First of all, in approaching my client in this way, in receiving her and in automatically feeling the nonpersonal Divinity (that is, a Divinity that did not belong to her or me), I formed a relationship with her on a human level that quickly became very deep. God is never far away from such intimacy. Holographically speaking, this relational intimacy was a small portion of the way God relates to us—namely, with utter closeness. Separateness is our primary illusion. God is so close that we miss seeing the Divine. So in receiving the Divine already in her, I saw the Divine already in myself, even though that was not part of my mission, and I grew closer to her, living in Reality what I had only thought about before.

Because Reality is self-similar, this small piece of intimacy within me was a fractal repetition of the larger Intimacy of God that I lived in and of which I was made. I had, in other words, touched the universally available quality of closeness, a quality that makes creation possible as it mutually co-arises in the relationship between the transcendent and the immanent. As we remained in that state of intimacy, through a kind of effortless-efforting—for it takes exquisite effort to truly see that effort is not necessary—her body began to feel the centrality of God. Faced with God, she could not help but heal.

God says, "I am everywhere," which is a law so simple and fundamental that when matter is faced with it, it holographically contains the seeds of its own liberation, as if each piece of matter has imprinted within it a map of the way home.

I have often said that if we could do this simple healing deeply enough, with enough informed faith, we would need no other Integrated Kabbalistic Healing. After all, as the Amidah, or Prayer of Eighteen Benedictions, says, "Heal us, O Lord, and *we will be healed!*" When God is Present, there is no question. Yet we know from experience that at times the Healing of Immanence is not enough, and that certain problems respond more effectively to other kabbalistic healings. Why is this so? How does this healing, which is infinite in nature, get limited by us, and how is that limitation made manifest?

To understand this, we must go more deeply into the nature of a universe that is truly holographic and self-similar and see how the very notion of communication changes in a situation where everything is seamlessly connected. Do the same rules apply when there is such depth of connection, vertically and horizontally? How do we understand the notion of action and reaction, cause and effect, doing and being, subject and object, when there is such interconnectedness as to make all things One *and* separate simultaneously? When we see how one small thing can change an entire system, the notion of communication as transmission seems inadequate.

Understanding this will help us understand God better and the reasons why communication with the Divine realm is both so easy and so difficult. Glimpsing the marvelous continuity within the created world enables us to see how each of our actions has untold repercussions, and how both what we know and what we do not know have an impact on the world around us and our relationship to it.

MAKING REALITY

We should not confuse Reality, with its limitless and eternal qualities, with what we are capable of understanding and seeing. Instead, we need to see that human beings pull out of the plenum what they can relate to, what they already are. We are made in a certain way, so we perceive Reality in a certain way: Reality truly is what we make it. Our eyes see only a certain part of the spectrum. Our bodies are of a certain shape. We live only so long. We all want happiness. We all have imperfect parents and psychic and emotional pain we try to bury. Usually these limitations are hidden, and we no more notice them than we notice a body part that is not currently injured and working as it should work. We simply go on being.

When we are not clear, when the force of our historical pain still holds sway in our lives, then the stories we make about the world and ourselves reflect that pain in many different ways. But when we have done enough historical investigation, we become clear-sighted enough to see the origins of that pain. Then by understanding these stories, a path opens up that allows us to get closer to the truth of the wholeness of our lives. The cleaner the mirror, the more it reflects what is.

Of course, even when we see a glimpse of the Light, the soul that is not yet ready to see in a non-split way cannot hold on to it and sees only its own reflection once again, its own small self in another disguise.

This means that we make Reality over in *our own image*. This is not blasphemy, but the human way. And it is because of this human way that both neurosis and its resolution can exist. In other words, we are neurotic because we cannot see the whole picture and generalize what we do understand to be true for all of life; and we can heal because God gave us the possibility to see our limitations. Seeing our limitations is how we touch the Infinite, not by becoming the Infinite but by embracing the limited. With this embrace comes the potential for kindness, generosity, and connection to the worlds around us.

How is it that those who have penetrated the Mystery of Being from many different traditions can talk with each other as brothers and sisters, reveling in the identity of realizations as they respect the differences among their approaches? The answer is that people who have broadened their ability to see various dimensions of Reality can understand others whose experiences are similar. They are more connected to Reality, to God, and therefore to each other.

This broadening happens not only in the arena of mysticism, but in the give-and-take of everyday life as well. When we see others as having the same hopes, dreams, fears, and sorrows as ourselves, we automatically feel closer to them; we feel that they have a similar worldview, and that they can be understood as they understand us. The Greeks and Turks—who have had long-standing animosity toward each other—suffered disastrous earthquakes several years ago. The Greeks were among the first to send rescue workers to Turkey. In return, when the Greek earthquake hit, a team of Turkish workers arrived within hours. This exchange probably did more to help the relationship between these two ancient countries than years of meetings in the sterile rooms of commerce buildings. They saw each other's suffering and humanity.

They shared in the joy of finding people alive after being buried for days. The Turkish rescuers were greeted with joy in Athens and vice versa. Only time and courage will tell if these two peoples can continue in this way without the need for tragedy.

The spiritual path appears as we move out of our limited view into a broader view. It is primarily a change in attitude. The first hallmark of having attained some level of the "awakening," or true connection to God, is the understanding that we have attained little and that, for the most part, we are still seeing our own face in the mirror of life. This is always the starting point.

We are like small ships on a vast sea, trying to understand its shape and depth from the single vantage point of our boat, hanging on the side of one small wave among multitudes of waves. To see God's image instead of our own is the work of the spiritual path. This perception brings understanding. To see how and where the two images—our personal self and the transcendent self—coincide is wisdom.

Let me be blunt: there are no objective sephirot, there is no actual Etz Chaim. These are inventions of the human mind and soul and are our response to the Infinity that is the Intimate One who is everywhere, the faces of this Reality that we can see and make sense of. New paradigms often bring us deep insight, but not because Reality changes; we are drawing a new piece out of the Whole. This piece is still not the Whole, and we should not mistake it for that, but it can point us in a new direction. Our new paradigm tells us that it is the self-similar, holographic piece to which the human being can relate. When we are thirsty, we do not need a river; we simply need a glass to dip into the river.

In the instructions for the Healing of Immanence, we ask people to "receive the already-in-existence Divinity of the person they are working with." Because we each pull out of Reality what we are, this statement means many things to many people. What we end up pulling out of the river is ourselves. As a consequence of seeing ourselves in this way, coming face-to-face with who we are, our most intense effort goes into understanding *who* we are and *why* we are. As we have seen, this is the work of Yetzirah. Once that work becomes firmly entrenched in us as a way of being in the world, we continue with the work of Briah, which is the work of residing in the holographic nature of the universe. It is the work of surrendering the ego's dictum that it is the only valid center around which we can know Reality, so that we can know the will of the One Who Resides in All Things.

THROUGH DOING AND BEING

Both the work of Yetzirah and the work of Briah are done so that we may change our hearts. We accomplish this change first through doing and then through being. Finally, we do it through the unification of the two, where doing and being are seen as two sides of one thing.

We do this work because when we are engaged in a relationship with the Truth, we are less likely to stop the Light of God. Simply by being willing to be open in this way, we become more transparent and can exist in God's Light without shattering our consciousness. The Light passes through us without hitting as many obstacles.

To those who have worked on their behavior (Assiyah), states of feeling and meaning (Yetzirah), and their ability to be in nonduality (Briah), the act of doing the Healing of Immanence—seeing the Divine in the person they are working with—is a transcendent experience in which both the healer and the one being healed share equally. There is no longer a separation between the two: Grace falls equally upon both. Our doing is completely in the service of our being.

And yet we are only human, and no matter how long our life is, we can never finish sweeping the stable and straightening the room. There is no end to doing. If "finishing" was what God asked of us in order to be with us, God would have no companions, since that work is never done. In fact, from my perspective, to see that form of purification or "finishing" as the goal is to miss the point.

Our individual consciousness was born—to invoke the metaphor revealed by the seminal kabbalist Isaac Luria—from the withdrawal of the Ayn-Sof and the creation of the Vacated Space, which is the very division into "God is *here*, but not *there*" that the Shema tells us is impossible. So the fact that our individual consciousness exists is a result of an incomplete picture of what is really going on, an illusion.

But seeing that this is an illusion is only half of the journey. The other half says, in effect: "While it is true that God is everywhere and that there is no place without His Light, it is also true that this so-called illusion has yet a deeper truth embedded in it. This truth is the truth of being human and seeing God's Hand and God's Heart within the condition of separateness." In fact, the Mystery of Being is not completely understood until both the Oneness of Unity and the Oneness of Duality are known: the Holiness of the Absolute and the Holiness of the Relative, Heaven and Earth.

Our preference for either Unity or duality—God or God's creation—interferes with our capacity to see all of God's truest kindness toward us. Glimpsing this kindness, however, will help us to understand why God created separate beings and, through that, to comprehend the deeper meaning of compassion, love, service, and prayer. This is the still deeper perfection inherent in this imperfect realm. God has placed the whole in each piece, and everything that is, is holy.

The journey to this level of realization takes place in the context of a universe created by God that has a level of interconnectedness that can be appreciated only when we have stepped off the pedestal of the separate-*only* ego and looked with fresh eyes.

When we begin the spiritual path, many of our problems—the things that separate us from other people and from what we understand the Divine to be—seem overwhelming. We see them as a succession of separate things: our relationship, our sexuality, our selfishness, our laziness, our lack of feeling, our anger, our resistance to effort and our resistance to *non-effort*.

As we continue on the path, we begin to see that some of our problems can be grouped together. Our lack of faith in God might have its origins in our distrust of our own being; our distrust in our own sense of self might have its origins in our fear of our anger; our fear of our anger might have to do with our inability to accept imperfection.

We begin to see patterns in our story and this recognition makes it possible for us to narrow our focus and, paradoxically, to place more of our pain under one rubric and work with it more effectively.

The fact is, if we have a problem in one area of our life, we have a problem in many. Because of the holographic and self-similar nature of things, our difficulties are not linear in nature, limited to "here" or "this." They are always global. If we have a problem with trust, it will show up with our mates, our children, and our God.

As we understand the interconnectedness of our difficulties, we also can gain an important advantage. Working on one area of our life affects all areas of our life. For instance, as we work on our personal relationships, becoming more genuinely trusting in that area, our trust in God automatically increases as well. The reverse is also true: as we learn to trust God more, we can trust our personal relationships more. In addition, as we learn true trust, we become more able to distinguish trustworthy situations from untrustworthy ones. This lets us become more resilient, and survive the times that trust is broken.

From this perspective, *we* are changing and *we* are opening to God's world. But because God's Intimate nature is expressed through-out the universe, the movement from above complements our move-ment from below. We are joined by Grace with the whole of ourselves as soon as we move in that direction. Like a bead of water tracing its path down a window, we join with other beads of water and eventually form a small rivulet moving toward a larger stream.

Martin Buber tells a story in a small pamphlet called *The Way of Man:*

A Hasid of the Rabbi of Lublin once fasted from one Sabbath to the next. On Friday afternoon he began to suffer such cruel thirst that he thought he would die. He saw a well, went up to it, and prepared to drink. But instantly he realized that because of the one brief hour he had still to endure, he was about to destroy the work of the entire week. He did not drink and went away from the well. Then he was touched by a feeling of pride for having passed this difficult test. When he became aware of it, he said to himself, "Better I go and drink than let my heart fall prey to pride." He went back to the well, but just as he was going to bend down to draw water, he noticed that his thirst had disappeared. When the Sabbath had begun, he entered his teacher's house. "Patchwork!" the rabbi called to him, as he crossed the threshold.

Why were the Hasid's genuine spiritual heroics derisively called "Patchwork!" by his teacher? Buber says that the disciple's spirituality "was not of a piece." In other words, it was still conceptual and did not arise from his Wholeness.

He was still taking an assiyatic approach to the problem of human fragmentation. While that approach shouldn't be diminished or put down in any way, it is important for us to recognize that he did not yet understand the nature of the central player in his drama of separateness. As a result, he was trying to work piecemeal, pushing this way and that, only to find a never-ending supply of things to work on. The rabbi obviously wanted this student to make a leap: a leap from noticing the parts to noticing the Whole.

When we notice the Whole, we see that it is intelligent and can be trusted to take us further into Reality, into Nearness with the Name of All Things. It is then that we have a chance to experience the Intimate One, the One who gives and takes, who is always in relationship with us.

Because the world is holographic and self-similar, everything that God does affects us and everything we do affects God. How is this possible? How can we affect the Eternal One? The One who Created? The One who is Beyond creation? The answer to this question is the answer to the riddle of our being alive and conscious in the first place.

Why is it that, faced with the almost insurmountable difficulties of being human, we maintain against all odds our desire to be happy, to find peace, and to establish a conscious relationship with God? Why should we even think for a moment that there is something better? Is it simply a matter of remembering an imagined "golden childhood," where all of our needs were met? Or, if we see through that illusion, a "golden womb-hood" where all our needs were met?

No. It is because there is something "of a piece" that resides in each person's soul—in fact, in the soul of every created thing. And this something remains no matter what. It is God. It is the Real Self, our original face before our parents were born. It is God in God's expression that God is everywhere. There is no place devoid of God. God stands at the bottom of our soul. God *is* our soul. God is the very reason we can exist. Our Real Self is nothing but who we are.

Meister Eckhardt said: "The Eye with which I see God is the same Eye with which he sees me." The Seer of Lublin said: "Patchwork!" Both these fellows knew something of the Whole. The rabbi was asking his disciple to trust his united soul, the presence of God, rather than his idea of God and the spiritual path as a kind of bouncing from one trouble to the next, from one adjustment to the next.

All of these ideas come into play when we do the Healing of Immanence with its simple instructions: "Place your hands upon the person and receive the Divinity that is already within him—which you do not have to *bring* to him, since he is already That." At this point, we have the hologram of God's world and the hologram of our own world. Every piece of our separateness comes into high relief, and every bit of God's Unity is there too.

We, as healers, must fall back upon our humanity, which stands at the crossroads of creation: part Earth and part Heaven. At first, we do our best to become "more holy," but then we remember the mission: "Simply receive the already existing Divinity in this person." So we step aside. But this stepping aside cannot be stepping into trance or oblivion. Instead, we must be present as God is present. We must be holy as our God is holy. Eventually, we even allow ourselves to come and go, no longer needing to be a certain way. Day and night, night turning into day, and it all is good.

It takes time to do this work of integration and not shatter, not resist the Light with self-judgment and self-flagellation. It takes practice not to see in our limitation a diminishment of our self-worth, and instead to see within it the cause of our celebration and life.

Doing the Healing of Immanence is the art of being human, of letting God's Light pulse through even our darkest spaces. It is the combination of doing and being in action, the getting-out-of-the-way and the acceptance of what is. This divine dance allows us to see the person before us in glory, and the ultimate victory of being a Real person in God's world comes closer, like a morning sunrise.

And whether we are healers, which is to say specialists in helping others, or simply people on the path, the description of the Healing of Immanence is the description of the spiritual path itself.

Doing this work, either with others or simply with ourselves, we make up fewer stories about God and the world and the people in it and we begin reflecting the world clearly in its magnificence. From this perspective, we cannot help but bow down.

QUESTIONS AND ANSWERS

Question: Could you say something more about the difference between being and doing?

Jason: Yes. Sometimes people come up to me with the thought that they should "just be." There is a prejudice for "just being" because we are so interested in countering our deep desire to always *do*. But being in that way is not any better than doing. It is still a polar opposite. It is still *reactive*. It might be a good antidote to overdoing, but it is still yetziratic work, since it involves a certain type of choice, made in reaction to a perceived problem. The briatic state would be that state where being and doing are the same thing, where being has doing in it and doing has a feeling of being in it. This is something entirely different. In this state we could actually choose being over doing or doing over being and not be ashamed of it, knowing that our choosing was holy and not an escape.

The danger in even talking about this is that the more we talk about it, the more exotic and desirable Briah seems. Then our poor egos, which are constantly suffering, begin to look to "magical" Briah as the place our suffering is erased, never to return. For the sake of helping our poor deluded egos to avoid this particular trap, I'd like to point out that we enter the world of Briah when we are not fixed in any one place. This means that we don't have preconceived concepts about what is going on. When we are not fixated, we become part of the process instead of something that is a secondary description of Reality: a thought, in other words, and not Reality itself. You could identify me if you wanted to. You could say that I am a bearded, bald fellow of such-and-such an age, but none of those things would be true. All the descriptions of me are not who I am.

FIVE

Within Death

Sitting in silence with Marilyn on the phone, I was in the face of death. In that face or presence, nothing I could do, think, or even feel was sufficient.

First, I had to go through the narcissistic stance or conundrum: Do I feel enough? Should I feel something different? Shouldn't I have a revelation in the face of this pain? Shouldn't it be teaching me something? What does Marilyn need?

Throwing all these thoughts up against death, not one of them survived.

There was no "me" that I could use to do anything or help in any way. There was no feeling that could help. What Marilyn was interested in was my presence, and anything else was bogus. Death kept forcing me to be more transparent and to give up any "stance" or personal position or even personal question: "Should I be this way?" or "What should I feel?"

The tidal wave of death washed that away. But an awareness, a hum, remained. And that was what Marilyn was interested in and where it was difficult for me to go. My ego only wanted to build edifices. Death didn't want to tear them down: it was supremely uninterested in any thing.

What was left in that silence was Who we both were. This was hard for the ego to accept because there was no self-reflective one to feel it. It was simply Presence and Light.

—JASON SHULMAN

*When my mother was dying, I realized that she was no longer
the person who was "mother" to me. That was not what she
was interested in. That special look in the eye she had for me
wasn't there. It was not that she didn't love me, but that she no
longer had that definition. She was something else.*

—ARLENE SHULMAN

DEATH STANDS LIKE A MASSIVE LIGHTHOUSE on the horizon of
our lives and flashes back a message we have trouble understanding.
And yet all of our lives are illuminated by this dark light, and people
live their lives—unconsciously, for the most part—in reaction to the
approach to this place of ending.

Historically, death has been discussed primarily from two vantage
points, which kabbalistically we can term the worlds of Assiyah, or
action, and Yetzirah, or formation.

As we have seen, these worlds are the universes of our everyday life:
the world of cause and effect and behavior and the world of the psychological,
symbolic, and historical aspects of our lives. These have
been the primary ways and the principle languages we have used to discuss
our concerns about death, and the confined vocabulary associated
with these worlds has limited the scope of what it is possible for us to
see and understand regarding this subject.

So, we have assiyatic clinical discussions and yetziratic ethical discussions.
When does death begin and life end? When can we transplant
organs? Do we have the right to "grow" organs in cloned beings? Is there
a difference in the death experience for different socioeconomic groups?

The philosophical questions have been deeper still. How can God
give us both life and self-consciousness and then allow us to know that
someday we will cease to be, that the world will go on but we will not?

Some people have had insights of great power about death and dying
from the yetziratic point of view. These understandings have been powerful
enough to penetrate all the universes. Yet when those insights are
communicated in the languages of Assiyah and Yetzirah, they do not
transmit a new way of being; we are not taught how to make those

insights our own. We read stories about sages and masters who died embracing death and we say, "Oh, I could never have that level of faith!"

Death stays a puzzle to be solved only by the very few. It remains not so much a Mystery with a capital *M* as a mystery with a small *m*, a moment of confusion and despair that does not lead to deeper insight but to greater aloneness; that does not bring us closer to God's world but makes us fall back on a memorized faith that is a substitute for true love or wordless knowing. We become diminished. These deep questions affect our personal lives, our families, and society as a whole.

My purpose is not to offer thoughts from these already articulated levels of understanding. I am not talking here about the suffering of dying or dealing with grief or loss. I primarily want to add a view of death from the universe of Briah. Here the notions of subject and object break down (or are subsumed) into something greater. I feel we must ask, "*Who* is it who dies?" And if that "who" changes its identity from kabbalistic universe to kabbalistic universe, then what we think about death and being dead must change too.

Kabbalah teaches us that we need to be free, free enough so that our small will becomes identical to God's larger Will. We keep ourselves from this freedom by not understanding the many dualities in our lives, by not resolving the conflict we feel within ourselves between all the great opposites of this world: love and hate, individuality and surrender, courage and fear. But even when we courageously work through many of these eternal themes, the last great duality—between life and death, which each human being owns equally—remains as an existential and fundamental barrier to our unification. In other words, we cannot be finally unified without resolving, to some degree, the question of death.

BEYOND THE FEAR OF DEATH

Imagine what life would be like if you did not fear death. The great yet-ziratic lesson regarding this subject is "Live each day as if it were your last. You do not know how long you have, so minute by minute, work out your life with diligence and kindness." The great briatic understanding is "There is no death. Nothing is born and nothing dies. Go about God's business."

If we could understand and live out both of these understandings, wouldn't our lives change? The journey to understanding and living this insight is personal and global; it will affect both individual consciousness and cultural perspectives. What need would we have of ponderous institutions whose secret purpose it is to establish our immortality if we learn that in truth we never die? What need would we have of dead traditions—that is, traditions that are used to coerce people—if we were not afraid about our own ending? Then tradition would be free to be wisdom, and institutions free to serve. We spend half our lives trying to live and not die. In this way we die and never live.

But for those of us who are willing to walk the road of being "so awake" now—who feel compelled on some level to put ourselves in God's Hands—we have an exciting future before us. As D. H. Lawrence said, "We need to prepare our ship of death," in order to live most openly, most warm-heartedly. This new knowledge of our own life and death awaits us. It is our birthright.

We are after "something else" in our view of death, and to get a glimpse of that, we need to leave the usual ways of thinking and re-vision this piece of human life from a new vantage point, a place where all opposites rationally and logically end, where love and hate, consciousness and nothingness, death and life, are part of a greater Whole. God never leaves us. We simply have not known what God looks like in this silent land.

Life and death are always together, and it is our psychic blindness that separates one part of this intrinsic Whole from another. We need to dare to take the view that death must be present alongside us for there to be life. We must also understand that God does not bring down this so-called great enemy upon our heads only to injure us. What is His way? Why is there death? Does it signify anything? Is it an end? A beginning? And how can *we* personally know anything about it?

If we do not investigate life and death from this vantage point, it would be as if we were medical researchers observing hands dissected from a body. Though we could intelligently infer that a severed hand could once move and hold things, was once warm with life, we would never actually see or experience these things since the object of study was an isolated appendage.

Our understanding of death has been stunted by our fear. For the most part, we have examined it only from the vantage point of Assiyah and Yetzirah. From Assiyah-only, we see that the one who lived ceases to exist. This much is obvious. From the perspective of Yetzirah, the psychological world, the emotional impact of death is often overwhelming. We have grief, sadness, loss, and other profound emotions with which to deal.

Our usual understanding does not include the briatic point of view, so we do not have the whole picture. In a very real sense our old, narrow perspective is severed from what is actually happening. We have no direct connection to El Chai, the Living God beyond life and death, and we cannot understand why the Source of our self injures us.

The Kabbalah is uniquely suited to address this question. Not only does it contain a highly comprehensive worldview, one that includes all the universes of creation, but it also teaches us that we must have the courage to look at everything in human life from every angle in order to truly serve the Source of Life.

It is my hope that a new way of understanding death, when embodied in people, will aid in the relief of suffering. It will not make the pain of loss go away, but rather put it into a context that is understandable, rational, and verifiable by personal experience. It will let us learn by personal experience that what is alive cannot ever be otherwise.

But like all transformative experiences, these new insights will require the reader to cease to be a reader and instead become a traveler, an explorer of conscious living, someone who is willing to be awake through the hard times as well as the good times. In essence, I am saying that the reader needs to become a participant and—through this relational process—become the crucible of his or her own proof of these ideas.

I am not now speaking about "what happens on the other side." What I really want to talk about is the connection between the living and the dead. Because if death is truly a part of life—and this is not some idea to which we simply pay lip service—then as any creation in this universe, it must add something to the Whole. It must have a reason, even if that reason is the destruction of reason itself for some yet higher paradigm. If death is truly part of life, we should be able to make use of it in our daily lives; it should improve the way we live; it should make us better people. It is my hope that these words will help do that.

GEMATRIA

The process of transformation can be aided by one of the methodologies of Kabbalah known as *gematria,* a traditional method of Torah exegesis. Gematria is the science of assigning numerical values to Hebrew letters in order to reveal deep associations and meanings, seeking to make clear actual, often hidden, correspondences among ideas, insights, and even physical objects that on the surface have little obvious connection. It sees each letter as an element in a series of perspectives that are enfolded into the appearance that Reality finally takes.

Unlike most other languages, which have their origins in Yetzirah—that is to say, the world of symbols and associations—Hebrew has a totally consistent structure based on the briatic is-ness of the thing-in-itself. For example, in English, letters are basically symbols that stand for sounds. While the letters of the Hebrew alphabet similarly stand for sounds, each letter is also essentially linked to a condition or quality—that is, each letter *is* a condition or form Reality can potentially take. These "conditions" are the building blocks out of which the universe is made. Thus the letters of the Hebrew alphabet can be seen as units of creation, with creative potential in and of themselves.

We can gain a deeper understanding of this by remembering that biology sees all life-forms as being derived from the sequence of only eight basic elements! The different amino acids are created not by new chemical compounds, but by the arrangement of eight primary bases. These eight bases are responsible for the creation of all proteins, and—folded and arranged in special ways—all of the genetic code. Similarly, the infinite variety of forms in this universe can be seen as arising from the arrangement of the twenty-two letters of the Hebrew alphabet.

This implies that the individual conditions, or "consciousness," that correspond to the building blocks (the letters) existed prior to the Creation of the universe. From this perspective, these "letters" "pre-exist" the creation of duality—that is, our world-itself. Our world, ourselves, all, spring from this fountain.

Thus the first letter of the Hebrew alphabet, *aleph* (א), stands for such conditions as unity, power, stability, and continuity. This is true in all cases; every word that contains an *aleph* has these conditions embedded in the essence of that thing or action.

The second letter, *bet* (ב), embodies the conditions of interiority, of dwelling, as in dwelling in a house. It is the place primal energy can dwell. In Hebrew, every word that has interiority as its main preoccupation contains a *bet*.

As an example, we can look at the first word of Genesis, *bereshit,* which begins in Hebrew with the letters *bet* (ב) and *resh* (ר), the twentieth letter of the Hebrew alphabet. While the aforementioned *bet* exemplifies interiority, *resh* exemplifies movement, the head, or the beginning of a new enterprise. Fabre d'Olivet, the author of the seminal nineteenth-century work *The Hebraic Tongue Restored*, likens *resh* to the radius of a circle that produces the circumference. So *resh* is the figure of *potential creation.* In this way, the first word of Genesis takes on new meaning. If we drop associative thinking and, in the Pure Present, consider this word, we actually begin to *feel* the power it has and its place in creation. In other words, the word has power within itself.

Because of this, gematria is much more than a method for finding psychological associations or poetic correspondences between different words—as valuable as that might be. The relationships exposed by gematriac analysis are primary, since they are, in a sense, instructions for creation rather than commentary after the fact.

To clarify this distinction, it will be helpful to recall the difference between associative relationship—which is concerned with the symbolic associations between words, phrases, and concepts—and the type of consciousness found in Briah, which I term intelligence of the heart (after Schwaller de Lubicz), hieroglyphic consciousness, or the consciousness of the Pure Present.

While symbolic or poetic associations are quite interesting and add a degree of depth and fluidity not possible to touch by simply reading words, this type of association is still at the level of Yetzirah—psychological space—and therefore is still conditioned by the invisible assumptions of that world, one of which is that the source of thought and what is beyond thought are not reachable. In Briah, this unreachability is not the case.

In essence, what is beyond or beneath thought is invisible in Yetzirah. In Briah thought is seen for what it is—memory operating in the Now, layers of history covering a dynamic and free world, God's world. Just as the addition of psychological insight enlightens and completely changes the action and behavior-oriented world of Assiyah, Briah's quality of the Pure Present radically changes the insightful world of Yetzirah.

While it is possible to maintain the illusion of intellectual objectivity when studying from the perspective of Yetzirah, in Briah we are asked to change, so our ability to perceive is changed as well. A parallel to this is the well-known fact in quantum physics that the act of observation changes what is observed. There are even indications—as described in the work of Princeton professor of aerospace sciences Robert G. Jahn—that this happens at macro, observable levels of the world as well. How we are, in other words, seems to affect how the world is, or at least how deeply we can see into it.

At the briatic level of inquiry, unlike with earlier or less integrated levels of inquiry, subject and object must disappear or be reduced in order for understanding to emerge. This briatic approach to gematria begins to make sense only as we ourselves enter briatic consciousness. Until that point is reached, all references to a briatic approach are conjectural and imaginary. When *we* change sufficiently, however, this new perspective unfolds with obvious clarity.

Gematria offers us a dynamic way to enter Briah, functioning as a tool for penetrating into deeper and deeper levels of Reality, including death.

THE DEAD

Said R. Shimon: "Woe to the man who says that the Torah merely tells tales and ordinary matters. If this were so, we could compose, even nowadays, a 'torah' dealing with ordinary matters, and an even better one at that! . . . In fact, all the words of the Torah represent lofty themes and sublime mysteries."

—ZOHAR

"Faithful are you, who raises the dead."

—THE AMIDAH

The phrase "the dead" appears in the Amidah, one of the central prayers of the Jewish daily ritual, also called the *Eighteen Benedictions:* "He sustains the living with loving-kindness, resurrects the dead with great mercy . . . [and] . . . Blessed are you, Lord, who revives the dead."

Using gematriac methods that have been developed over centuries, some of the numeric correlations to the word "dead" or the phrase "the dead" in Hebrew are:

entire
whole
wholehearted
without blemish
expand
shall enlarge
my birthplace
in the entrance
beautiful
complete
a gift (as in "the gift of water from the Wilderness")

Why should these words and phrases somehow be hidden in the phrase "the dead"? Stated another way, why should the energy and consciousness found in the letters that make up the phrase "the dead" reappear in these other phrases and words? And finally, what is revealed thereby?

"The dead" in Hebrew is written: המתים. Read right to left, the first letter, *hey* (ה), stands for the universal life principle. This letter and its interior principle also show up in the spelling of the Hebrew words for "breath," "soul," and the phrase "idea of being." The letter *hey* can also be associated with the concept of "wall" or "enclosure" and with outward-moving, vivifying, and animating conditions. Expanding on these meanings, *hey* can be seen as the animating condition in its enclosed or protected form—that is, the spirit in form. This is true whether the *hey* appears in the word תהיה, "exist," or the words האר, "to brighten," or הארה, "brightening," "illuminating," or "clarifying." Grammatically, *hey* is also the definite article *the*.

The next letter in the phrase "the dead" is a *mem* (מ). As with the others, this letter embodies a basic form of consciousness, part of which is the productive, fertile, creative source, associated with water and woman as origin-places of creativity.

When *mem* is combined with the next letter, *tav* (ת), we get the concept of death. To quote from d'Olivet: "If one considers this root as composed of the sign of exterior action, united to that of reciprocity, or this same sign joined by contraction to the root (מת) image of the ipseity, [selfhood] the selfsameness of things, it will express either a sympathetic movement, or a transition; a return to universal seity or sameness. Thence the idea of the passing of life; of death."

The letter *tav* (ת), which alone has the meaning of the completeness of life, both in its possible perfection and in its completion in death, when combined with the next letter, *yod* ('), leads to the image of the depth of universal existence and the feeling of being lost in empty space.

The final letter combination contains two letters, the aforementioned *yod* and *mem*. *Yod* by itself stands for "eternity," "duration," and "potential manifestation." When it is combined with the final *mem*, we get the conditions of "manifestation united to that of exterior action," or "universal manifestation."

Thus, the phrase "the dead" has within it these energies in a sequence that indicates the pulsatory movement of life from one sequence or state to another. We can read these lines as a poem death writes as it continues to manifest life while undergoing transition to a new state.

[Enclosed and brightening]
/the outward-moving animating life energy/
[Enclosed and brightening]
/fertile and creative Source/
/selfhood—passing— transition—selfsameness/
/exterior/
/depth—void/
/new manifestation—ongoing creative principle/

Within the numerical lineage of these words also lies the word *tumim*, meaning "completeness." This word is used to describe the vestments worn by the high priest, specifically an elaborate and bejeweled breastplate with a pocket into which Moses would place the written-out ineffable Name of God. This Name, composed as it was of the living letters, was a Completeness or Whole, and was by implication the answer to all questions.

This *constellation of motive forces* combined with the words and phrases that are *gematrically* linked to "the dead"—such as "wholehearted," "entire," and "whole"—are the "the dead" I am talking about: the dynamic movement of life energy, at first enclosed in an individual, then moving, transforming itself through the mystery of death, and finally manifesting again.

This is death in its *unfolded* form, and it is only by entering Briah that *this* notion of death can come to light and a new understanding emerge. Of course, entering Briah means existing wholeheartedly in Assiyah and Yetzirah—that is, surrendering to the human conditions of physical death and its emotional consequences.

Because we are talking about a language from which duality emerges rather than a language formed from duality, what we are seeing here is the interior, unfolded nature of "the dead" and not conjecture.

This understanding is the embodiment of Briah, and entering Briah we are no longer talking about theory: briatic discourse has the feeling of cement, of rock and stone. It is from Briah that certainty and the belief that is not the opposite of doubt, but that stands alone, arises.

My hope here is not to teach the discipline of gematria, but to report back my findings. Even without a personal understanding of gematria, the truth of death can be found by any individual willing to truly look at the world. Our entire world is a message: it is only death that sustains life. The suggestions and myths of life after death, ubiquitous throughout every culture and time, offer more than the psychological denial of the end of human life; they express the subtle sense we all have that *something goes on, something continues.* The idea here is not to believe blindly but to work at belief. What does it do to infiltrate our notion of what death is with these words?

[Enclosed and brightening]
/the outward-moving animating life energy/
[Enclosed and brightening]
/fertile and creative Source/
/selfhood—passing— transition—selfsameness/
/exterior/
/depth—void/
/new manifestation—ongoing creative principle/

We can use these words as an anchor to hold steady in the sea that contains life in death, death in life.

THE WORLDS OF LIFE AND DEATH

"'Male and female He created them.' From here we learn that any image that does not embrace male and female is not a high and true image. . . . The Blessed Holy One does not place His abode in any place where male and female are not found together. . . . A human being is only called Adam when male and female are as one."

—ZOHAR

All of Reality lies invisibly within nested pairs of manifested opposites, which lie in each other's arms, inextricably linked. Reality is not about *things* but about the indivisible *relationships* between things. It is only when we deny this intimate Wholeness, tearing these lovers apart, looking at these facets as if they had a purely individual existence, that *things* appear. Then the Wholeness that lies within is lost to our sight.

Objects and things disappear to the extent that we are involved in intimacy. When we are intimate with What Is, the Whole appears, unbounded and infinitely deep. The Whole can be described as an enfolded or nested completeness.

In actuality, we usually see pieces of the Whole, which presents many faces or sides—known in the Kabbalah as *partzufim,* or "countenances"—to the ordinary mind. We might see these faces as units of relationship the way "mother" is the name of a relationship that exists only because there is a simultaneous, though unnamed, counterpart called "child." In actuality, the observer pulls out of the nested Whole those elements that the method of observation, whether mechanical or psychological, can apprehend. When the ego is given the "supreme position" in consciousness—despite the fact that it is not a whole, but a fragment of consciousness—it elevates these parts to a kind of pseudo-whole. This is an invention of the ego that mistakes these things for something real. The real Whole, which is the source of these faces, or pieces, waits in silence beneath appearances to be discovered in intimacy.

These partial manifestations have utilitarian uses, however, for beings who live in the illusion of separateness. The illusion of complete identification with the separateness is strongest in the universe of Assiyah, the three-dimensional universe of our daily life, a universe in which time moves only from past to future, and the spiritual realm is a distant memory of a mythic, golden time.

In Assiyah, the ego in its completely separate state still exists. There is no real interiority or unconscious; there are only different types of behavior. Assiyah is a sensate world where the seemingly separate observer of the world is the master. We do not have the experience of an interior psychological space until the ego is faced with a potent example of a realm over which it is not in charge. In other words, the ego needs to be confronted with a "hiddenness" before it allows the concept of limitation to exist. Something happens, or some feeling emerges, that the ego cannot explain away; some failure of control occurs.

Interiority exists in Yetzirah because the separated and observing ego—which thinks it is a whole but is really only a part—is no longer completely convinced of the supremacy of its own vision of things. Luckily, however, through the agency of doubt, a deeper truth begins to leak through the limited vision of Assiyah. We might say that the Wholeness takes the form of doubt as it tries to break through our illusions.

The world of Briah—which recapitulates Assiyah and Yetzirah—adds its own dimension. Because this universe is the home of something more essential than either of the two previous realms, it is not concerned with things, neither exterior things (such as in Assiyah) nor even internal things (such as in Yetzirah). Instead, it is concerned with relationship as its main understanding. Briah is the realm that is always concerned with both halves of a polarity and the "third thing," the Invisible and Silent thing, of which they are both faces. In Briah we are interested in the paradigm of the nest itself instead of the things that go into making the nest. In this new way of seeing, nothing is left out. Everything is in relationship in one way or another.

In Briah, both the inside and the outside—whether speaking psychologically, physically, or any other way—are of equal importance.

One is responsible for the existence of the other. All thoughts, good and bad, are simply "thoughts." The appearance of duality gives way to what is within this appearance. We no longer need to save ourselves from Wholeness.

In Briah, past and present and future are seen contemporaneously. The Absolute and the relative are seen as different facets of the Unnamable. Even life and death are seen and experienced as two sides of a single coin. We begin to experience them simultaneously. Life, with its manifold descriptions and constant movement and change, is seen as existing within death's category-busting essence. "What exists" is seen anew in the light of "no ground," "nothing," "without," "empty," and "boundaryless."

The Prajnaparamita Sutra, also known as the Heart Sutra, perhaps the central exposition of the Buddha's transcendent wisdom in the Mahayana tradition, expresses this condition of unity in the following way:

> This radical teaching of truth is openly presented as a nonteaching. Therefore, nothing can obstruct this teaching, which is as all-embracing and ungraspable as space, no trace of which can ever be found, crystallized, isolated, divided, tested or analyzed. This teaching of truth is not related to any other teachings, because it does preserve the concept of otherness, nor does it encounter any adversarial positions, because it does not proclaim any principle of opposition. It is a traceless teaching because it is utterly sponta-neous—not brought into being by various causes or influences. (The One) now speaking has never been born . . . (but is) an image of Pure Presence . . . (he is) the image of the One who has disap-peared by awakening as Reality. . . .

When Rabbi Shima Bunam of Przysucha was dying, it is said that his wife burst into tears. When he asked, "What are you crying for? My whole life was only that I might learn how to die," he was speaking as one for whom death was not the opposite or destruction of what he was. Instead, he saw clearly who he truly was. His true unification lay in the unity of his life and death. While in this story they are presented as sequential, in Reality, life and death are always simultaneous, twins whose existence creates what we call "the Now" of our life.

In Briah, time and eternity are one; the temporal and the atemporal are one. Rabbi Nachman, the great sage of Breslov and the author of the magnificent *Likutey Moharan*, said:

> If we look truthfully at the loss of time and see how quickly it slips through our fingers, leaving us not a moment's rest or peace, we will see that time really does not exist. It is but an illusion, resulting from the limited nature of our minds. Similarly, in a dream, one can imagine that seventy years have passed but then, upon awakening, realize that it was only a quarter of an hour. . . . Recognizing the unreality of time, one understands that it is futile to be caught up in timebound hopes; one should rather aspire to that which is beyond time. And believing in this category, "beyond time," one will never fall; for all falling is a function of time.

But how do we get to this exalted understanding? Although Reb Nachman's description uses the language of Yetzirah, his accomplishment was consummated in the mansion of Briah, and that is where we must go to live for ourselves the Life in God that is beyond both life and death.

ENTERING DEATH

It is a kabbalistic certainty that steps cannot be skipped on the journey to the source of our being. We cannot—by will or talent—arrive in Briah legitimately without going through the work of Assiyah and Yetzirah.

The initial work of Assiyah is to become safe with the physical realm, to sort out our various behaviors so that we can begin to see what truly furthers our interest and what does not. Assiyatic work also consists in beginning to bridle the ego so that it can be ridden to the next level. But we cannot do this without the work of Yetzirah, which teaches us why we are unsafe. The work of Yetzirah is the work of uncovering our history: the words, images, feelings, and memories of our personal journey from childhood to adulthood. This archaeological expedition into the *unthought known* is the primary step in human evolution. It is here that we encounter *the hidden* that, like the pea under twenty-three mattresses, still disturbs our sleep. In this case, of course, "the sleep" is our life, and the process we go through is noticing how we re-create our early childhood wounds in a doomed effort to come to homeostasis and health.

Doing the work of Yetzirah, we move step-by-step from our personal history—which is always in memory in that it is in the past—into the Present Moment, a place where we are not conditioned or captured by the past re-creating itself again and again in our present lives. Doing the work of Yetzirah means that when this history appears again, we are no longer enthralled by it. Slowly, through often arduous work, we begin to learn how to remain present for longer and longer periods.

But yetziratic work does not stop; it is the *halacha*, or "path," that we must travel. "Entering Briah" simply means that a shift has taken place and that we see that the problems we face and the solutions and resources to overcome them are all within us. It also means that we have the stability—the healthy egoic strength—to stay centered as we are pushed and pulled by the karmic winds of unfelt pain and their handmaidens: transference and projection. We might call this new state "faith," but it is a faith tested by the fire of remaining "seated on our base" as the world around us whirls.

This is the stage of work where no one can "do" anything to us anymore, nor can anyone save us. We might say we are diligently working out our own destiny, or we might say we have put ourselves in God's Hands. At this level of "who we are," either characterization is accurate.

As R. A. Schwaller de Lubicz puts it, "we are no longer standing *outside* the Temple *pointing to* the Temple, but are *within* the Temple." Then the "Temple"—which is ourselves, our difficulties and our greatness—no longer exists as an object of desire or contemplation. It is no longer separated into "things," and we no longer see our path as a series of "patchworks." We see it instead as the series of nested opposites of which Reality itself is made. Then our life is a true House of Learning, a true Wholeness, as any temple should be. And because this Life/Temple is unfragmented and has an implicit integrity, it can help us take the pieces of our heart and put them back together. The world becomes a worthy doctor. We are then more free to just do the work we were sent here to do.

When this realization dawns, the endless, internal conversation and history-making machinery within our souls begins to quiet down. We find ourselves in relationship, which is to say, not in experience. At first only in moments and later more steadily, experience quiets down, and there is no one left to comment or chastise, criticize or judge. We still do the work of Yetzirah and purify, but it is within the context of this larger perfection, beyond time and opposites, beneath the appearance of things, in the middle of effort and ease. We meet each new event in life not as a stranger, but as a new facet of the Great Friend.

This is the type of relationship we need to have with death: not standing outside it and pointing to it, but standing within it. What does it mean to be within death while still alive? As a start, it means throwing everything we do up against the paradigm of the final ending, not only, as in Yetzirah, so that we can feel the preciousness of every moment, though that is absolutely necessary. It is rather so that we can experience bodily what it is like to have the freedom of the largest context of all.

This is the state of Oneness the Shema talks about—it includes opposites and is beyond opposites. In this state, one never acts solely out of concern for the future or past, since time has been erased. Fear is both an illusion—since the one who feared is no longer there—and something that exists within the same moment. In this context, there is no loneliness—since the one who is lonely has disappeared—and, paradoxically, loneliness still exists, indeed is *allowed* to exist fully and vibrantly, since there is nothing one holds on to that opposes loneliness. A new thing appears in the world, ever new, whenever we allow these opposites to take their place in each other's arms. We might call this "new thing" a sage who has no enemies.

What is the personal self or historical self like in the palace that is beyond the personal? In this state of the nondual present, the person is completely free to be in memory, no longer identified with memory as being one's very Self. Such a person is equally free *not* to be in memory since he or she exists not as an experience but as part of the nested Wholeness that makes up That Which Is. This state of death-in-life allows both the personal and the impersonal to exist without question. This palace of death allows consciousness and what is beyond consciousness to exist as equal partners.

In this place, which is another of the mansions of our Maker, we stay with death as a brother or sister—not gruesomely, but vividly. We stop trying to save ourselves from "the end." We allow "the end" to be already here. We are beyond "the end." We allow the frightening things, the "shards" that prick us and hurt us, to remain within our consciousness, neither escaping nor holding them to us. We hold our congealed difficulties within ourselves, neither burying them—thereby creating more history and more karma—nor acting upon them— thereby creating more "behavior."

Then, by the divine law that says that there is no place devoid of God, these fragments, or *klipot,* show their true nature and return to their source. They resume their "original face" and become an ally; they take the form of the original Light instead of a separating darkness, a Light that *includes* darkness and is not opposed to it. To quote from the fourteenth-century Sufi master Shaikh Al-Arabi Al-Darqawi's letter to one of his students:

> As to this professor you told me about who is unable to find the
> state of presence, tell him not to look toward the past nor toward
> the future, to become the son of the moment, and to take death as

the target before his eyes. Then he will find this state, God willing.
. . . We said to one of our brothers: Let him who wishes to be in a
perpetual state of presence retrain his tongue. And we advise you:
if you are in a state of perplexity, do not hasten to cling to anything, either by writing or by anything else, lest you close the door
of necessity with your own hand, because for you this state takes
the place of the supreme Name; but God is wiser. Ibn 'Ata-Illah
says in his Hikim: "Sudden distress is the key to spiritual gifts";
and again: "You will perhaps find a benefit in distress which you
have not been able to find in fast nor in prayer"; therefore when it
descends upon you, defend yourself no longer and do not be concerned with searching for some remedy, lest you drive away the
good which comes toward you freely, and give up your will
entirely to your Lord; then you will see marvels. Our Master used
to say when someone was overcome with dismay: "relax your
mind and learn to swim."

What the Shaikh describes is in the spirit of the work of Briah. Once we
enter this new land, none of the old landmarks disappears. Instead, a
new relationship is illuminated, and through that, everything is
changed.

DEATH IS THE PAIN OF THE WORLD

Death is the pain of the world because all created things hate to die. To
die is to submerge part of oneself, to slip consciously into an openness
that does not protest against pain or the changing world.

Whenever we—without self-pity, but with an awakened acceptance—
say, "This is the way the world is," we are dying: dying in the way a
wave sinks back into the ocean, tired of its momentary existence, exul-
tant at its moment of height, and accepting of the loss of the kinetic
energy that kept it aloft. It sinks downward into the ground of its being,
hanging together by gravity for a little while, and then shift upon shift
spreads out until it is not a wave but an outline of what a wave could

be, and then even less, as some of its substance is raised up as part of another wave, with another purpose, another life and death, another timing and another rhythm. It is picked up, momentarily put down, and picked up once again.

When we remain whole and see the laws of this world, we die. We die because the true laws of this world, God's laws, do not favor one side or the other, but only Wholeness: the Wholeness that is beyond description or conflict, that has only truth as its center. True laws are always the centers around which the opposites of this world orbit.

When we see our blindness and that of others around us, and we neither exclude ourselves from it nor partake of it, we stay alive and die at the same time. It is like laughing and crying at an event of great significance. We then feel alone, even as we lean on our companions, who we know feel alone as well. We signal to them as if across a vast distance, as close as brothers and sisters yet infinitely far.

As we let go of "opinions," a piece of the world disappears. But this piece was only a piece, and a piece—no matter how many of them are put together—can never be a whole. So a piece disappears. It drops out of sight into a wholeness. At first we panic a little. We keep looking for who we *were*. Sometimes, much to our bad luck, we find him or her, and return briefly to our old home and try to set up a life that is already leaving us. Eventually we let even that piece fall away and then we are completely dead. And being dead, we are free to live, and we catch glimpses of others throughout history who have found the same thing, and the currents made by their arms and hearts, their feelings and form, thread around us and we sing to the stag in the night, the wild beast who of its own accord comes down from high fields to graze with the flock, but who maintains its wild nature and its wild and original mind.

Death is the pain of the world and also the recipe for its Illumination. It makes the slight, glinting beauty that consumes us. It makes every moment precious and sad. Then living and free, we don't hesitate. We stop and look.

I hope with all my heart for a future world where the attitude and experience of death has been greatly changed, one where the dead themselves are seen anew and alive. Not "alive" in a superstitious sense, as spirits that haunt the living or even act as guides—newly minted channels and sages who advise the living in matters pertaining to life— but as one with us in the continuity of God's world.

I hope for a society where the fear of death is tempered, not by fantasy, but by certainty. This alone would teach us how to live. I envision a future where we understand how large the Unity is that God operates from, a time when our small faith has been expanded to *knowing*, a relationship with certainty that is beyond dogma or fixed ideas.

QUESTIONS AND ANSWERS

Question: Do you think that actually can happen?

Jason: I don't know. Reaching a new level of understanding about death requires exacting personal work, great honesty, and a level of impeccability that might need several generations of experience to settle in before the culture would begin to trust the new paradigm.

But you can experience some of what I mean right now, by trying the following two exercises. Try them faithfully, which is to say with your whole heart, setting aside the mental debate that might arise. Let them settle into your being and then see what occurs in your body, mind, and spirit.

Try this. Imagine, for a moment, that the best minds and hearts of humanity have determined, *once and for all,* that after you die, you are simply and irrevocably *dead.*

There is no Heaven.

There is no Hell.

There are no angelic realms.

There are no after-death dreams, or at least not any that outlast the final destruction of the body.

There is no one there to reward you *or* punish you.

You may not realize it, but many—if not most—of your actions come from holding on to a dream of the afterlife. If you were not a subtle and learned person, you might act in certain ways so that you would be rewarded in Heaven with money, or pleasures, or eternal life. But because you are subtle, the rewards you are looking for are subtle. You want to know more about the universe, and you believe that after you die, you will know more. God will tell you and show you. You believe that the pain you might be in now, whether physical, emotional, or spiritual, will be allayed, that something will happen that will take it away. And you do good on this Earth in order both to avoid punishment and to find your way into Heaven.

If you have any doubts that you feel this someplace within yourself, simply and silently repeat to yourself: "They have really, really, *really* found that nothing exists after you die." See how you feel. Contemplate this. Take it as true. It *is* true. What will you now do with the rest of your life? How will it change your actions, feelings, and thoughts? Don't say "It won't" too quickly. If you find the way in which it does change you, you have a chance of entering into Briah.

The purpose of this exercise is to bring us blindingly into the Present Moment, to let nothing stand in the way of our arrival on this plane of existence, not even the future promise of fulfillment.

And try this as well.

Whatever you think you are, allow it to die.

Your name does not exist.

Your family does not exist.

Who you think yourself to be is gone.

You have no job or career, or even religion.

What is left? Can you feel the *hum* of Something within you? Keep still.

Now you are breathing, but one day you will not. Does this *hum* disappear?

"Ask" the *hum* what it is. Listen to the answer.

Anything, no matter how "holy," that is not in the Present Moment can ultimately keep us from the Divine. In this way, eventually even the so-called holy, when misunderstood or misused, can become an obstacle, keeping us from the palace of the One Who Made our heart. We cannot do only yetziratic work and expect a miracle. We cannot do only briatic work and expect a home. Life without death is not alive.

When we are capable of vividly holding opposites within our body, which is to say not only as a mental construct, but as a sensation or sense of physical knowing within the body, the "third thing" that frees us appears as a gift. We prepare a place for this gift through our personal, historical work, our commitment to the process of this work and our love. But our work is not finished until the moment we say, "Life and death are One in God," and bring these two poles closer and closer within our mind and body until they merge. Then a new freedom, palpable and alive, is born.

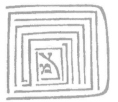

SIX

Prayer: The Concrete Path

Prayer is meant to be a direct line of communication with the depth of our heart and the height of our soul. For us to pray, all that is needed is that we speak. But prayer—one of the most vital ways to experience God—is also a way that has become petrified. Having been handed down a form of fossilized prayer, many of us have lost our way. We have forgotten that our lives are the prayer God chants, *and that these same lives can be filled with God's longing, God's promise, God's fulfillment, and God's glory. The Kabbalah offers us a way to live in prayer, as it transforms every practice, taking it out of memory and into the living Now.*

NO PRACTICE IS SO MISUNDERSTOOD or so little used as prayer. Nobody actually ever teaches us how to pray for ourselves, how to put *ourselves* into our prayer, how to make prayer a ceaseless current that takes us to our destination. Prayer has become so dead in so many ways that we don't even know fully *why* it works; its workings have devolved into superstition: pray *this way only* and God will hear you and respond. We search for the formula, forgetting ourselves. We think that we *already* need to have faith to pray, when in fact prayer is the greatest means to find the faith we think is missing.

When we feel a sense of deep connection, we seem to understand how the universe works and what our place in it is. We then say we are "connected to God," or "experiencing ultimate Reality"; we speak of "is-ness" and "*de'vekut*-cleaving." The names and descriptions are much less important than the experience. It is that moment of connection and wholeness that we are looking for, and not the word itself.

In fact, when we are connected, we don't call this "state" anything. It is only afterward, in retrospect, that we look back and say, "Oh, I was really connected. I felt the presence of God." Or, "I felt the source of my being." Or, "I felt my Buddha-nature." In the moment of connection the connection itself is nameless, the Nameless One. It is the connection *without* a name.

Although this wholeness is part of our birthright and belongs to us, we all lose it. To regain it, we do our practices such as prayer. But we never know exactly when or whether our practices are going to connect us to the Real; it is as though we are usually blind, waiting for the bolt of lightning to strike. We don't know what it is that changes us. Some people wait for lightning to strike, and others wait to wear away the infinitely large stone that stands as an obstacle between them and God. We don't know exactly why Heaven responds and why Earth responds, how to put Heaven and Earth together, or what the dynamics of this interchange are.

For many of us, the very thought of praying becomes a problem. Since we don't know how to do it, we find fault with ourselves: "Our prayers are not passionate enough; we don't have enough belief; our intent is not strong enough; our prayers are selfish." We end up feeling more alienated and alone instead of more connected and wise.

When we pray, most of us are casting a message in a bottle into an unsure sea. We don't know what to write the message on. We don't know how to put the cork in. We often do not even know if there *is* a sea to carry our message, or in which direction the shore lies, or if there are truly currents that will take our bottled message to the One who can read the letters of our heart. Ultimately, we often end up wondering whether there is even One there who reads our hearts and listens to our words.

I would like to explore this issue of prayer in a very practical way so that we can actually see how the universe responds to our call, not in theory but in real time, and so that we can use this vital practice once again to bring us to Life, to God. I want to share a way to approach prayer that we can work with on a daily basis. This approach is based not on reading from a book of prayers, but from reading our own hearts and learning to give voice to those inner words.

This practice works with our sense of separation and allows us to connect with the Divine no matter where we are, physically, psychologically, or spiritually. It takes into account that prayer itself exists because there is separation between ourselves and the Almighty. Because this understanding is at the very basis of this type of prayer, there is no state of mind, no condition of the heart that is beyond the pale of this practice; we do not need to be whole in order to pray. In fact, this approach to prayer helps us see that within our very separateness—which we take to be our fundamental problem—is the root of liberation, the heart of Wholeness.

ROAD MAP FOR THE SEARCH

This approach to prayer is deeply grounded in the Kabbalah, which offers us a wonderful road map of the process of unification. It is one of the most insightful descriptions of Reality that has come down to us, through the hard work of men and women who loved God and wanted to know God heart to heart. The Kabbalah describes the way the universe, the world, humankind, and human psychology work. It helps us to understand what the Shema implies—that even though we all lose the sense of wholeness and connection, the wholeness we are looking for is already intrinsically ours.

If we can understand the kabbalistic description of Reality properly, which really means that we *participate* in the understanding this description brings, it will illuminate our search for truth and help us enliven every moment of our existence. It will help us work with the difficulties of everyday life and bring us a sense of connection. And it will allow us to work with life whether we are in the heights of joy or the depths of despair or someplace in between, where most of us are most of the time.

In fact, if the Kabbalah *is* a good description of how Reality works—of how God interacts with us—it is going to have to work with *all* of those states and not be something that works only with some special state, such as those moments when our faith is confirmed, or when we have been hurt enough by life that we can finally accept anything with grace. By working with the entire gradient of human experience, Kabbalah will show that it is a trustworthy friend, a teaching of life itself and not of the theory of life.

One of the later developments in Kabbalah was the understanding that there is subtle and endless dimensionality to our consciousness. As we have seen, this dimensionality was expressed as the four universes, which are simultaneously a topographical map of the levels of Reality and a statement about increasingly integrated levels of Wholeness. The schema of the four universes came out of the experience of the mystic explorers who began to understand the organization of consciousness, the nature of God, and the nature of prayer. This schema offers us a grammar of Reality that allows us to make sense of our experience by placing each of our actions and practices up against a wider screen, to see better how they relate to the whole. In this way we can clarify our view of Reality and unmask aspects that appear to be one thing and are actually something else.

The four universes are *points of view* that give us new insight and perspective on every aspect of our being: from our physical form to our psychology, from the way time flows in the universe to the way life and death intertwine. They are a way to talk about what happens to us as we heal and integrate the split and broken parts of ourselves. They are a way to talk about what life will be like when that happens and as it happens. They are, in a sense, a description of the spiritual path, moving from separateness toward union and with a new understanding of what that union really is.

Because we all have egos and because this will always be true for us as human beings, all so-called spiritual work is actually work on the ego. What I mean by the ego is the abiding sense of separateness that we all experience, from the voice inside our head that tells us what we think to our separate bodies and individual feelings. This separateness is at once the foundation of our individuality with its possibility of growth and a troubling feature in our makeup that leaves us without a direct connection to something beyond our small self. When we are not connected to this "something," we feel alienated from Heaven and Earth.

Yet this ego, this sense of separateness, is the vehicle that allows the spiritual journey to happen. Our relationship to it is not an obstacle to our journey, something to get rid of, but rather the entire content of the journey. The ego is not to be discarded in favor of some fantasy state where we are free of the ego, "Free to be you and me!"

The spiritual journey is about healing this separate sense of self: not healing it out of existence, but letting it truly be part of existence, part of the Whole. Without this sense of separateness, which is also the seat of our identity, we are nothing. With it—when it is unhealed and broken by the weight of misconception—we are also nothing. But when it is healed, it is the vehicle that connects us to the deepest source of satisfaction in ourselves. Illuminated, it is the gatekeeper to what we most prize: the connection between Heaven and Earth. It is beauty itself.

This is true because the healed ego, which might be called a *personally held* version of pure awareness, is not a purely personal thing. It not only belongs to us personally but is also held in common by all sentient beings; it appears in every aspect of the manifested world. We might call it an *urge to be*. The healed ego is the voice of the universe, calling to us; it is that portion of the Whole, of God, of Buddha-nature, that we carry around, not only as owners, but as caretakers too. When it is healed in us, the world looks different since we no longer see through limited eyes. We then have the possibility of freedom, of what sages in the past have called liberation, awakening, enlightenment, or God-realization.

On a *personal* basis, the urge to be takes on different forms depending upon which part of ourselves is holding it, or which screen it is projected upon. In other words, it doesn't have a central location, like the Freudian idea of the ego, which is only a part of consciousness. This urge to be manifests in our body, our feelings, and our mind. It takes in our history—such as our birth family conditions—and even conditions *before* we were born, such as our genetic endowment. It is found in the part of us that seeks something more out of life, even when it is weighed down by troubles or ignorance. The journey of spirit does not occur to wipe away this separateness but to see *within it*, so that we are able to see our truer, deeper connection to the All and not only the separateness itself.

We are here not to abolish separateness in favor of something else, but to add the something else to our separateness so that our lives are richer because they have a greater context, a greater scope, and we have greater understanding and the possibility of wisdom. We want to be able to understand that both our separateness and our connection to the All are valid and holy.

The spiritual journey changes everything because the world we see is really the world *we are* at any particular time. So the journey through the four universes describes *how we change* and, in changing, see the world differently.

First we see the river and study the river. Then we see the shore and study the shore. Finally, we start understanding that the river and shore form an inseparable whole, and that rather than one of them coming first and the other second, they arise together, each of them creating the other as they go along. This new level of study, which we might call *spirituality*, helps us return to the undeniable fact that all life is One, that we belong here although we suffer, that we are made to be here, though we also die.

We need to *re*-vision ourselves so that all of us can come into being, the small parts and the mighty parts, the weak parts and the wise. True spirituality is not a new thought or a new feeling; it is a global change in attitude and conception. It takes hard work. Although spiritual literature is filled with stories of these changes happening "all at once," like a flash of lightning, in no case does that actually happen. It is simply that sometimes the preparation for this new state of consciousness happens in hidden ways, and even in previous existences.

As we journey through the universes, we will begin to understand why the ego arises in the first place. We will also begin to understand that its intent is holy. I want to underscore that the ego is never lost or discarded throughout this journey. Rather, it is held in kindness and healed, and the story of these universes is the story of that healing.

PRAYER THROUGH THE FOUR UNIVERSES

The first thing we must understand is that there is no one thing called "prayer." Prayer is an activity that we approach from the state we are in—that is, the condition our ego is in. In reality, there are as many types of prayer and praying as there are people. And while all of them are acceptable to God, if we don't know what type of prayer we are engaged in, we can mistake one type for another. We cannot understand the answer to our prayer if we don't know the question we were asking. Most of the time, we do not have contact with our entire being but only part, usually the most conscious part. But it is all of ourselves that prays, and when some part of a prayer-filled person is unconscious or hidden, the creation that issues from that prayer is unconscious as well. We can end up creating unconsciously, never understanding the result.

So to understand prayer, we need to understand *who is praying*. The kabbalistic idea of the four universes explores the transformation of this *who* as we grow and change by the practice of prayer itself. By looking at the three kabbalistic universes that have to do with human relationships, we can see what happens to the human ego in each of these realms of integration, and see how, as the sense of self changes, it changes the world. (The fourth universe—which from the holographic point of view is concerned with the ultimate realization of God's presence, the *action* of the enlightened and transparent view on the physical plane of existence—will not be considered, since it is beyond the scope of what we are discussing here.)

Prayer in Assiyah

As we have seen, Assiyah—the universe of *making* or action—is the one closest to our everyday, three-dimensional reality. It is, in a sense, a physical place, where the separation of all things is highlighted: you are here; I am there. In this realm, we are also certain that this thing we call a "self," our ego personality, has a continuous existence from one moment to the next. We see this self as a real and concrete thing, as solid as a table or chair, yet, paradoxically enough, in danger of annihilation at every moment.

The diagram below is a representation of the ego-consciousness in Assiyah. It will allow us to understand some of the attitudes about self and world that come from this level of belief and being.

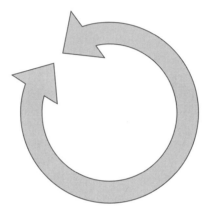

Figure 6.1. The ego in Assiyah

The implications of this diagram are many. The first thing we notice is that here consciousness is looking at itself. It is completely self-referential and self-reflective. When consciousness sees only itself, the sense of self is completely separate from everything that is *not* the self. In other words, subject and object are completely separate. In Assiyah-only, when it is not connected to the rest of the universes, the ego is not yet well developed or well rounded. It neatly divides the world into what gives it pleasure and what seems to hurt it.

To go even further, since this form of consciousness sees only itself, it is truly interested only in its own destiny and survival. This has profound implications for our behavior, because from this point of view all behavior must ensure the continued existence of this self, just as it is. The ego in Assiyah is so self-referential as to be almost at the level of instinct. Since there is no "thought," per se, mental activity takes the form of the almost automatic sequences that are needed to keep the existence of the individual in perpetuity. We never question the existence or rightness of the self, but are more concerned with how this self makes its way in the world: who supports its existence and desires and who stands in the way.

The universe of Assiyah is the world of "action"; everything in this universe or level of awareness is about *action,* and what we *do* is the most important thing. This world is tied to the physical in that actions are deeply physical things; we express ourselves physically. Since all of reality is physical, even time is experienced in the most linear fashion, as flowing in only one direction, from past to present. The ego feels itself to be continuous in time, and therefore bound to time as well. As a consequence, the ego fears the passage of time and sees it as presaging its own end.

Here we have a worldview in which the solidity of the material world—and all that implies—is taken for the absolute, entire truth. Our pursuits to meet our physical, emotional, and spiritual needs take on the characteristics of this universe; the physical becomes the metaphor by which this world is guided. Just as in the physical realm everything is specific and locatable, all the differences or locations between things are highlighted. Things that cannot be physically seen or understood, such as the spiritual worlds and God, are believed to be far away.

Strictly speaking, there is no unconscious in this world, since there is no *interior* or anything hidden that is seen to be *within* the self. There is no "interior" in which to find "inner motivation" for our actions. Our actions are all simply to ensure our own survival. The ego is used here to create solidity and existence and to fend off anything—idea, person, feeling—that threatens it. We still have our other faculties: we think, we feel, and so on. But all of them—until the ego is healed—are used in the service of solidity, continuity, and safety.

Spiritual work in this universe—when it is not connected to the other universes—is behaviorist: *Do this,* and these things will follow. But the *reasons* things work the way they work remain a mystery. In this realm, we cannot see the *direct connection* between the way the world works and us. In other words, since this view is so limited, we cannot see the true workings of spirit in its entirety. Life and death remain a mystery that *we don't control,* so we tend to promote a magical—which is to say unreal—view of the world. We use our creativity (drawings, spells, idols, and so on) to communicate with, effect change in, and placate the unseen powers that seem to be there.

Prayer in Assiyah is often designed to rescue us from life's suffering. It is an attempt to communicate with a physically distant God who may or may not be listening. We practice ritualized ways of being with God that other people have developed and told us are effective ways to communicate with the unseen Source of the world. Here we follow the structure of prayer without understanding its origin. Here we set the incense "just so" without knowing why; here the ritual itself becomes the magical object instead of what its intent points to. Here we pray by rote. Here we ask God to be on our side, as if people on the other side are not praying for God to be on *their* side! Here we bargain with God in a physical way: "I will give you two sheep if you give me no locusts!" The inner connection has not yet arrived.

It is because of this disconnection that *anything*—even the most liberating philosophy or practice—can be used as an *idol,* something that is used as an external and magical consciousness instead of a tool to increase inner awareness. For instance, democracy is a political philosophy that enhances the freedom of individuals. However, when it is turned into an idol, it can become the worst form of patriotism, which is often used to actually *limit* the freedom of individuals.

There are also profoundly *positive* things to be said about Assiyah, but these won't become apparent until we understand more about the other universes. Paradoxically, God is *completely* present in every universe, so the work that goes on in each is completely holy. But until we journey through the levels of integration possible in the other kabbalistic universes, the holiness of Assiyah must remain somewhat hidden.

Prayer in Yetzirah

We might call Yetzirah an intermediate state toward awakening and—though it causes its own difficulties—it is the creative space in which new, unheard-of levels of integration are formed. The perspective of Yetzirah makes a quantum leap into a new paradigm in which we dare to go into an area that Assiyah could deal with only by using superstition, magic, control, fear, and bewilderment. We enter into the world of the *unseen*.

In Yetzirah we discover the world of *internal* feelings and even the staggering concept that this interior world—which we call the unconscious—has many *undiscovered feelings*. In Yetzirah we realize that our conscious attitudes and thoughts sit on top of unconscious ones. We see that our interior life often keeps us from being in the Pure Present and instead keeps us in our history.

As we discussed earlier, the yetziratic ego looks at itself, so its shape is similar to the shape of the ego in Assiyah. But it is not completely engaged in the "trance of looking" that we saw in Assiyah, a difference that is reflected in the shape shown below.

The ego in Yetzirah is more fluid than it is in Assiyah. It no longer believes in its monolithic solidity in the same way and takes a more nuanced approach to itself and the world, trying to interpret the meaning of things. Subject and object are still separate, but no longer in such a hard-and-fast way. We see our connection with other people more clearly and deeply and learn how to have personal relationships as well, which is the foundation of movement to the next level of being.

In Yetzirah we begin our journey to the newly found interior of our souls. We sense that this place holds the key to the secrets of our self.

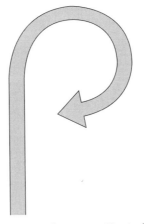

Figure 6.2. The ego in Yetzirah

Starting from our personal consciousness—shown by the arrow in the diagram below—this journey, from one part of ourselves to another, is represented by the dotted line that connects one part of the curve with the other, straighter part. The yetziratic consciousness senses somehow that there is a "Real Self," and it seems to "see" it "over there," as if it were a separate existence and not the curve of its own self. The yetziratic self feels it must journey to this mysterious place to find God or the Truth. Through this journey we see our fears, longings, and desires and get hints of how much we actually do not know, how much we are not aware of.

Through the work of Yetzirah, the ego becomes a vehicle not only for existence, but also for seeking. This leads us to question, to seek answers, to find out about ourselves. The quest to live a fuller life takes on a much different form than the assiyatic quest. Within this paradigm we want personal empowerment, personal enlightenment, and personal understanding. A healthier ego enables us to find out more about life in general, and our life in particular.

Yetzirah is the world of emotion, and it encompasses both the feelings we know about and the origins of our feelings, many of which are hidden from us. In yetziratic consciousness, we begin to see how our unknown internal desires act—without our *conscious* knowledge— upon our world, and for the first time, we see how we *participate in the way the world presents itself to our consciousness*. We begin to look for the origins of our feelings, undertaking the work of personal psychology.

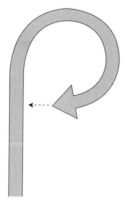

Figure 6.3. Journey to the Real Self

We join with others who are also searching out their hidden motivations and the enduring presence of the past in order to live freer, productive, and truthful lives. This work takes the ego to a new level of integration where we can have a personal inner and outer world. Even thinking yetziratically is an advanced spiritual condition, and without this process it is impossible to proceed in any authentic way. The world suffers from having so few people who actually do this yetziratic work.

Since in Yetzirah we still have spiritual needs, in this universe we become *seekers of God*. This quest takes the form of understanding the story of our lives more deeply. We feel that if we could understand the meaning of this story, our ego—which we still do not believe is our friend—would cease being something wounded that stands in the way of our happiness. As the methodology of the spiritual quest in Yetzirah is to understand our story, we make it an unconscious practice to stand apart from ourselves in perpetual self-reflection, witnessing our drama and commenting on it in order to understand ourselves better.

If we look again at figure 6.3, we see that the very act of self-reflection—shown by the bending of the ego-shape—is what creates our story. (The "space" for the story is shown by the dotted line in the diagram.) Since we are so entranced by the story and its meaning, however, we never realize that it is this very stance of separateness that creates the story in the first place; it is the *source* of the drama that the ego finds unbearable and seeks to remedy by the spiritual journey.

The final part of the yetziratic journey, which begins when we learn about the wounds of our past and how we carry them with us, is to learn about the *ego that stands apart* so we can finally put our wounds where they belong: in the past. Because of this *still separate* mentality, the universe of Yetzirah has its own version of Heaven. In Assiyah it was a mythical, physical place, like Valhalla or Shangri-La. In Yetzirah it is "empowerment," "enlightenment," "God-realization," or *de'vekut*—that is, God-connectedness or God-cleaving.

While these terms are more subtle, these vaunted states are still seen as being far away. In other words, we are still not in a state of God-connectedness *exactly where we are*, but must *do something* or *go someplace* in order to accomplish this goal. In this yetziratic world, there are still *two things:* ourselves the way we are and some other, better state. We have not yet reached the Oneness talked about in the Shema.

Prayer in Yetzirah is very different from prayer in Assiyah. In Assiyah, we have no tolerance for suffering: we pray to avoid suffering by doing the magical things we must do to avoid this fate. In yetziratic prayer we are willing—or at least *more willing*—to walk into our suffering. We are willing to do this because we have become spiritual adventurers, explorers of Reality who know that self-knowledge—and sometimes the suffering that goes along with it—is essential to becoming fully human. And although this view from Yetzirah-only is itself limited, this is a profoundly courageous thing to do.

In Yetzirah, our prayers take the form of dialogues, even if very often the other member of the duo is silent. A dialogue already implies that there is a different relationship between subject and object, one in which there is some actual communication between both parties. Having a dialogue means that there is an increasing level of integration and relationship. While God may still be invisible, we can *feel* the presence of God.

In Yetzirah, God seems to be both inside and outside; we seem to contain a portion of something that is vastly greater than our individual self. We begin to understand that we are indeed "made in the image of" God. Our prayers are prayers of inner need directed to the greater Source, but even this inner need is not quite so separate from God since we seem to have some of God within ourselves.

From the Assiyah-only perspective, we do not trust the universe to be generous and benign with us. We do not believe that God wants us to have every possible thing without our sacrificing everything that is important to us—our firstborn, our best fruit, our finest animal. In Yetzirah, however, we begin to feel that we *are* worthy enough for God to listen to, since we are somehow part of God. We still do not know why or how God will answer our prayers, but at least God listens. God listens and we talk. Someone now lingers, inside as well as outside. This is Someone we want to give our finest things to and not bargain with out of our fear.

The wonderful thing about prayer in Yetzirah is that we see God as a psychological friend who is going to help us on the level of our feelings. This allows us to have a personal relationship with God. "I have these feelings. I am so angry, God. Please help me with these feelings. I want to be able to love more." In prayers of Yetzirah we learn about how to work with faith. We also get answers *from* the past and answers *about* our past. "I have this pain from my childhood and I need to be able to forgive . . ." In Yetzirah we have the connection to the One who helps us with this realm, who can help us with the historical hurts we carry with us and which blunt our capacity to feel.

In Yetzirah we put our feelings into words again and again until—like a fire that burns up its own fuel—we are eventually able to see a new state, a state where feeling is not linked only to historical pain. The fulfillment of prayer in Yetzirah comes when we begin to see a place that *includes* feeling while simultaneously going beyond the only-feeling state. This progression allows us to see the need and possibility of praying from within the consciousness of Briah, the next most integrated universe, which includes Assiyah and Yetzirah and yet adds something new.

Prayer in Briah

In Briah we are an individual and *not*-an individual at the same time. While our assiyatic consciousness believes its physical solidity to be *the only* reality and our yetziratic consciousness discovers its own story as the heart of its consciousness, our briatic consciousness has no position to defend: it looks out and in equally. While time in Assiyah is only the "now" of the space between the past and the future and yetziratic time is of the "now" of the past, briatic time is all-at-one-ment, accessible, open, and never lingering.

Briatic consciousness does not "experience" the world in the way we experience it in Yetzirah. The ego-shape of Briah will give us a way to talk about this sublime state (see fig. 6.4).

The first thing we notice about this ego-shape is that it is an open-ended curve. It does not bend back upon itself. Second, we notice that there are no directional arrows; this shape is not tied to a particular vector or direction. Any belief or quality we attribute to the world of

Figure 6.4. The ego in Briah

Briah must take this shape into account. For instance, unlike the state of consciousness depicted in Assiyah and Yetzirah, briatic consciousness is not located in a specific place or space. The lack of arrows in the briatic diagram indicates that it is an open system that is not self-referential in the same way that the ego is in both of the lower universes. Only things that are self-referring can be said to have "experience" (something that is "saved up" and reviewed). Because Briah does not stand apart, but sees itself as completely part of the world, there is no one there to have experience in quite the same way.

Simultaneously, since briatic consciousness sees its separateness—its individuality—as completely valid, it also fully experiences the world as a human being. In Briah the ego is as valid as anything else in the world and exists for the pleasure of God. Of course, to even get to this level of integration, the ego has been deeply healed. The ego is not capable of taking its place unless it is healthy and whole. In Briah, the one who sees and what is seen are One. Oneness does not negate separateness, and separateness is not alien to Oneness. Therefore, in Briah we reach the stage at which the apparent conflict between separateness and the truth of Oneness is *nullified*. We are able to hold these opposites within our body, mind, and spirit. In Briah, even the existence of separateness—which automatically creates experience in the way described earlier—does not erase the existence of that greater thing of which *experience* and *no-experience* are part.

In Briah we no longer have to protect ourselves from the parts of ourselves and our life we do not like or are afraid of. This is because we are doing the yetziratic, psychological work of unearthing our history, taking responsibility for our actions, and allowing ourselves to connect with our true suffering instead of indirect or symbolic behavior. So we can, for example, feel our loneliness directly instead of creating a different form of suffering—perhaps a more acceptable form for our ego—such as overindulgence in food or various activities. When we resort to such symbolic behavior, we actually perpetuate the suffering since these preferred pains mask our true suffering. In Briah we face ourselves and our lives directly. This is our greatest task, and accomplishing it brings us our greatest safety.

Briatic prayer is prayer from the origin of prayer. It arises from the prayerful urge itself. When the first people put together the first prayer service, they undoubtedly chanted the prayers of *their* hearts, what was concerning them in that moment, their need to connect to the All in that moment. When anything is handed down from one generation to the next, it runs the risk of losing its original vitality—unless we who receive it have the courage to go to our own hearts and speak our own original words, without fear that certain words should not be part of prayer.

For most people, prayer is about reading sentences from a book, often in a special place set aside for that function, whether a chapel, a sanctuary, or some other sanctified place. And while we may allow many different types of feelings to enter our prayers in these places, we do not allow all of them; we censure certain feelings as unworthy of a prayerful or respectful attitude. People often mistake the concept of kavannah, thinking it means to have feelings of devotion, deep faith, or love. But while kavannah can have a devotional feeling, from a nondual briatic perspective, kavannah is really a form of focus, a practice of attention and presence. And when we have kavannah, all of our actions and feelings are prayerful ones. In other words, devotion is the God-connected state: presence with What Is. Then everything we do is simply a vehicle to express this kavannah.

Yetziratic prayers approached with the utter dignity that only kavannah can provide can be distraught prayers as well as prayers of gratitude, angry prayers as well as prayers of resolution, prayers of feeling lost as well as prayers of finding. Most important, however, yet-ziratic prayers approached in this way lead directly to Briah, because they are utterly honest.

In a briatic approach to prayer, a new possibility opens. It says in effect: "Start from where you are. The nature of God is to know our hearts, our secrets, our pains, and our longings. There is no need for a masquerade. We can never be perfect enough to satisfy the small ego's need for the illusory perfection that can protect us from all failure and from all of our suffering. But what we can perfect is our honesty. That is what we have to give."

The briatic approach to prayer calls on our utter commitment to honesty, even if we will inevitably fail from time to time in keeping that commitment. This is one of the most potent antidotes to our pride and separateness, the very things that keep us from asking for and receiving help. The important thing to remember in this approach to prayer is that *everything* is permitted; one does not have to be in a special place—emotionally or physically—to practice this. This, of course, is an invitation not to act out negative emotions, but to take full responsibility for them, while not being afraid of them.

Starting from where we are brings us directly to a briatic attitude and invokes one of the great mysteries of life: whenever we start in the place we truly are, we are automatically connected to the place we want to be.

Since this prayerful practice comes from the origin of prayer and is not concerned with reading an already established or published liturgy—prayers that were put together by someone else—it is a personal practice. To pray from a briatic perspective is the simplest thing in the world: it simply means coming out of memory and praying in the Now. It means being exactly where and who you are and knowing that this is all that is necessary to be invited into God's antechamber.

PRAYING FROM WHERE WE ARE

Briah contains and never separates itself from Assiyah or Yetzirah, and therefore in Briah our actions, our feelings, and our prayers are one thing.

In Briah our very actions become living prayers themselves because we are unified in a place where opposites are held in one paradigm—the past and the future, the fractured and the whole, the mundane and the sublime, Heaven and Earth—all exist in a relationship of complementarity.

Because Briah is not split by small-minded preference, we learn one of the great paradoxes of the universe: God is completely present in each separate thing. *All* of God is in Assiyah; *all* of God is in Yetzirah; *all* of God is in Briah. When we begin to embody this approach to life, there is something in us that responds. And no matter how far we think we are from fully integrating this type of consciousness into our daily life, just the act of our noticing the discrepancies between the way we are and the way we could be brings us closer to a truthful, God-connected way of living. We come to understand that God is not something it is possible to leave, that we live in God as God lives in us, *never come and never gone*. In other words, we come to understand that it is the *already-in-existence intelligence* that makes us seek this intelligence in the first place. God asks us to find God.

Both Assiyah and Yetzirah are concerned with *purification* and improvement. And in each of these worlds, in slightly different forms, the ego cannot yet be the holy vessel that it truly is. In Assiyah, we have only a part of the ego operating, a kind of psychological part-object. In Yetzirah, we are still trying to purify the ego—something that desperately needs to be done! At the same time, we are often trying to *get rid of the ego* because it seems to be the source of our pain. Briah does not have the limitation that either Assiyah or Yetzirah has. Its basic nature is *nondual*. Therefore, things that are a danger to our psyches in Assiyah and Yetzirah are *not* a danger to the briatic consciousness, but are the very way to "find" God right where God always is: here and now.

It is in Briah that the *healed ego* is brought back into the whole person for the first time, enabling it to become the chariot for the further work of awakening. Here we no longer need to sacrifice part of ourselves. Here we no longer need to stand apart, but are in the flow of life. Here in Briah we are safe *to have* an ego because the ego has been made safe for us and the world. It becomes our divine pleasure to have this ego with which to enjoy God's creations. There is no longer any opposition between ourselves and others. There is no longer anything shameful about "choice" or choosing what we want. We trust what we want because we know that all of life is divine. We no longer need to protect ourselves from anything that is "lesser." We use the world as God uses us, freely making the choices that move us inevitably toward Wholeness.

Since Briah enfolds Assiyah and Yetzirah and is therefore complete within itself, the healthy briatic ego does not need to "get ahead" or "get someplace" in order to feel at home. It is at home wherever it is. Briah seeks to see what is. Briah knows that what is, is *holy*. Therefore, the briatic view does not see the ego as a problem to becoming God-connected. It sees the personal self as a small but beautiful eddy, a tiny but important wave in the body of the great flowing river of existence.

Briah is not afraid of separation or so-called duality. Separation does not "ruin" its Oneness, but supports it. That is why, in a practice such as prayer, briatic consciousness is never afraid to start from wherever it is. Assiyah-only consciousness would ask us to leave our suffering behind, to be finished with it in some sense. Assiyatic prayers are about *not* suffering! Assiyah sees suffering as an obstacle to be overcome, and desires to manipulate the world in order to reduce suffering, which is valueless in and of itself.

Yetzirah-only consciousness sees suffering as valuable in that it points us in the direction of exploration: if we suffer, there must be a reason, and understanding that reason, which lies somewhere in our past, will help alleviate our suffering and thereby help us get to God.

To briatic awareness, personal, existential suffering is a fact of the world, part of the nature of separateness. It is a fact that should not be denied or manipulated. It neither needs to be sought out for spiritual attainment—as if the pursuit of suffering helps us in any way—nor does it *only* point to *personal, psychological problem areas*. It has transcendent existence.

Briah sees primary suffering *as something fundamental to this level of existence,* and knows that when it is allowed to exist, it becomes the very vehicle for our salvation because it is a truthful and real part of life. To briatic consciousness, everything that is, in the form it is in that moment, is holy. Even our partly understood feelings or thoughts, the pieces of us that are split off or wounded, the hidden parts of ourselves, even the misunderstood parts, are holy.

Prayer in Briah is beauty itself, and true beauty contains discord and ugliness, or what seems to be discordant and ugly at first. So a briatic attitude toward prayer asks us—above all things—to pray from where we are. This, of course, means accepting ourselves completely, even though we all suffer with the wounds of imperfect childhood and the wounds of this temporary state of being we call "life." This acceptance is the most important thing.

When we accept all of who we are, we "call out to God from Wholeness." Briah knows that God listens to Wholeness and that Wholeness is not some mythical state of perfection, but essential friendliness with who we are in each moment. And Briah also knows that when we are in a piece of Wholeness, we have access to all of Wholeness. Wholeness leads to Wholeness leads to Wholeness. In this way, we eventually begin to hear that God—the universe, our truest nature, our real self—calls us to Wholeness constantly, in everything we do and in every moment. Our life then can begin to be a response to this Calling, which is both our own true nature and the true nature of God.

When we pray briatically, we have the eyes to see the true form of Assiyah: Assiyah is the Holiness of the World. Assiyah's duality no longer frightens us; it is no longer seen as a place of exile. We see Yetzirah clearly as well, and our feelings, once freed of the "neurotic personal," become flowing and ordinary, seeing the miracles of this plane of existence—and its horrors as well—clearly and without shattering. Only in Briah do we see the absolute beauty of Assiyah and Yetzirah—Yetzirah as the palace of the personal and Assiyah as the physical abode of the Intimate One.

QUESTIONS AND ANSWERS

Question: What role do worship and tradition play for a person who has learned to be in Briah?

Jason: In such a state, it is completely different to say the words of the Amidah or the Shema, to read the words of Jesus, or to chant the Koran. For such a person, tradition may be a moment of immediate creativity, or a moment when past, present, and future come together.

We can also look at this question in another way: prayers and texts that last, that are divinely inspired, come from this briatic state of consciousness, a state in which the original author or receiver of the text is open to all of Life, no longer residing in the small story of an individual life *alone,* but opened to Life that is held in common with all beings. To then read these scriptures from a briatic stance is to reawaken the original intent and energy of the writing, is to join the past with the present Now so that the text speaks for the first time. This wipes the dust off the text and lets it live anew. It lets it continue its job of bringing the deadness in us to life again.

Question: Given what you've said, how do I approach praying? Where do I start?

Jason: It simply does not matter where you start as long as you start honestly and maintain your honesty every step of the way. The problem is not Assiyah, or Yetzirah, but Assiyah-only and Yetzirah-only. Staying in these states hinders the automatic and natural deepening that occurs when we pray.

I have often started my prayers in doubt or anger: "Oh, God, I don't even know if you exist. Why am I even speaking to you? I work hard on myself but always seem to slip back into difficulty."

If we start praying from where we are, what invariably happens is that the next moment, or the next day, whenever we continue our prayer practice, we are led from one universe to another. Once we do this we are on the ride for the whole journey. The very nature of Reality is that it has a sense of gravity, only this gravitational pull is always toward God. Because of this, as we let go, we fall toward the Divine. So I go from "I slip back into difficulty" to "Oh, God, this makes me feel so bad. Am I just not strong enough, or not applying myself enough? I don't understand it." This leads to my asking for help, to feeling my predicament.

Soon I am in a dialogue with the Lord of my being. Soon I am saying, or singing, since I actually sing my prayers aloud, "Thank you, God, for listening to me. I trust in your judgment to help me. Oh, let it be as it is. Amen, now and forever."

This "falling toward the Divine" may not happen right away, but it will over time, if we pray with honesty and the attitude of kavannah. An attitude of kavannah means to be present with each feeling, each thought, since each thing is important. Praying with kavannah not only *leads* us to God, it is simultaneously and paradoxically God Itself, the Whole contained in each piece.

If perfection is what is needed for us to reach God, we are out of luck, because we don't have the capacity for that kind of perfection. But we do have the capacity for honesty, and focused honesty is what we can bring to our prayer; it is that which moves us automatically from one universe to the next. Focused honesty means starting from where you are.

No matter who you are, no matter how many years you have practiced, no matter how "holy" you are, there is going to be a day that you wake up when you are filled with hatred, when you are filled with despair, or longing, or confusion. And then you have to say, "Dear God, I am so filled with poison this morning I can hardly get the words out. I can't even remember what it was like to be otherwise. And I even hate myself for having hatred." And that is your prayer.

Your prayer might stop there or you might find that it goes on, and you say, "So now I feel so hopeless, having said that, after all these years of working, I thought I knew something besides hatred and poison, but I see I have a long way to go. So now I just feel hopeless." Suddenly you are into the realm of hopelessness. From an Assiyah-only point of view, we might not want to be in hopelessness, but from a yetziratic point of view, *we do*. We want to have our feelings no matter what they are.

The prayer might stop there and if it does, that is fine. As long as you have been honest, it's fine. Or it may go on. "So now I feel my hopelessness and I realize that endlessly I have been giving myself a hard time. If there is one thing that I can count on, it is that I will always see the worst in myself. Why do I do that? I feel so much self-hatred for the fact that I do that. How can I ever get past this?"

And the prayer can end there or you may find that your kavannah of honesty, of starting where you are, makes a spark of something else come up. "Oh, God, I am tired of being this way. I don't know how to do it, but I have to have kindness for myself. I demand kindness for myself. Oh, there I am demanding things again. But I know nothing but doing that. I have to do that. At least I am demanding something better for myself. Oh, help me, God, to have kindness for myself. Even if it is only an atom of kindness, I know that like a single star in the blackest night, it will give me a place from which to orient myself so that I can find my way home."

Now, our ego, listening to this, will undoubtedly want us to go through all those steps to arrive at some reconciliation at the end of our prayer. Let me tell you—that is not necessary. It is nice if it happens. The most important thing is to follow, moment by moment, the flow of honesty. And you will not be able to understand this until you do it. And you will not be able to understand until that time when you wish you could go three steps and you are capable of only going one, and because you went that one honest step, your day was different, and your life was different. Not because of some hit-or-miss thing, but because this is the rule of the universe.

This is how the universe works. The levels of the universe are interrelated. They are not like layers of the onion where one is separate from the other. They interpenetrate each other. They are mixed, like a soup. A soup exists only because the potato gave its essence to the water and the water gave its essence to the parsley. The parsley gave its essence to the carrot, and we get soup. Soup is what happens through that cooperation and soup is what nourishes. It happens automatically when someone surrenders to who he or she is at the moment without pride or fear. That is what is necessary. That first time you realize that your ego is asking you to go further than you should—such as when you find yourself saying, "I am filled with hatred, oh, but God, I really love you, you are so wonderful and sexy," or whatever—when you come to the false self, the self that wants to fake it, stop.

That may mean that you will feel your separation and sadness more. What happens when you feel your separation and sadness more? You move from Assiyah to Yetzirah automatically. And you move from Yetzirah to Briah automatically. It does not matter if you still are sad, if you still are lonely, if you still say, "Oh, God, I want to know all the secrets of the universe, I feel this great urgency to know all the secrets of the universe and I feel so forlorn that I do not know them." If that is what your agony is, then being there with it will free it from you and you from it.

Above all, we want to do this in a practical way. We are not interested in creating a fantasyland. This is not prayer to feel good. *This is prayer to feel.* This is not prayer to make ourselves into something we are not. *This is prayer to make ourselves into who we are.* This kind of prayer is against the ego's vision of what the ego thinks it needs to be. In this practice the difficult has a home with the easy, the beautiful with the ugly, and what we see has a Wholeness that surpasses everything that is not complete.

One of the hallmarks of this approach to prayer is that you *must* say these prayers aloud—privately, but aloud. There are certain important reasons for this, not the least of which is that when we pray in our heads, in our silent inner voice, we often get confused as to who is speaking, which part of our psyche is in charge. But when we speak our prayers aloud, we hear them clearly. We *listen.* We listen and hear. It becomes even more effective if we sing our prayers to ourselves. There is no need for a great or moving melody: a simple lilting tune will do.

In Briah, prayer is to be where we are, when we are, as we are, without changing anything. It is that place where we fall into ourselves and say, "*Here* I am and *I* am here," both. Then like Abraham, we become the first Jew, the one of any religious persuasion who has an original mind and an original face, the one who cannot speak falsely.

When we can see that God made us for the enormous honesty that we can contain and not because of our perfection, when we understand that God loves us because we use what we believe is free will over and over again to find the truth—falling down we get up, losing our way we ask for help—then we will know that when we pray honestly for five minutes at a time, out loud, by ourselves, even the mightiest angel stops and listens, because it knows it is listening to a holy thing.

The Words of God

To grasp at knowing how we are to our Creator: Imagine the entire universe as a stream of conscious thought, and imagine how a single thought exists in its place of birth, within the depths of a Supernal Subconscious, a place before words, before things, where there is only One. We created beings cannot perceive the Source with our flesh eyes, and so we see a world. But to the Source there is no being, no entity, only the Infinite Light. Yes, we are here. But in the Higher Reality, there is nothing else but Him.

—THE LUBAVITCHER REBBE MENACHEM M. SCHNEERSON

Nothing's said till it's dreamed out in words, and nothing's true that figures in words only.

—LES MURRAY

In studying Integrated Kabbalistic Healing, a student learns the model of the Tree of Life, including a deep understanding of the sephirot, the *partzufim* or "spiritual countenances" within the Tree, and the associative pathways both within and between the sephirot. What emerges—when the student has begun embodying the work and not only perceiving it; integrating the work in wisdom and not only understanding it theoretically—is a healing modality and diagnostic process that maintains the Mystery of Creation while bathing that Mystery in the Light that has no counterpart. In this way the practice of healing itself becomes a spiritual path, transforming both the student/healer and the one he or she heals. Each healing the student/healer does is both a way of personal practice and a way of helping others: path and practice become one.

At the same time, this process of learning is filled with risk. It is possible, for instance, for students to believe that at some point they have this learning "under their belt," that they "understand the system," or have a fixed armamentarium they can call upon to give them the answers they search for. While we support and encourage mastery, the moment when living knowledge passes into the penumbra of remembered knowledge can sometimes pass by unnoticed, to the detriment of the entire program of personal liberation and healing. The teacher's job is to help the student avoid getting caught in his or her own ego's attempt to control the world, which reduces the shimmering aliveness of what we might call original wisdom to a stagnant concept, Life to an idea about Life, the great questions into small answers, and the healing path of Integrated Kabbalistic Healing into simply another modality.

Reading and studying Kabbalah, we walk to the entryway that leads to the unity of earthly and heavenly life. *Living* Kabbalah, on the other hand, we find we are Life Itself, as we always were to begin with. From this point of view, we must have the freedom to question and re-examine even our most basic assumptions and understandings: "Is this piece of what I know still alive, still relational, still dynamic? Has it lost something in the fight with familiarity? Has it settled down to a comfortable existence and lost the every-minute-kavannah or alive and present intentionality that is necessary to meet with God in every moment?" Thus it is with even the diagram of the Tree of Life itself. To enter into a moment of Light, we need to invite in a moment of confusion or not knowing. Every moment of creation is preceded by a moment of *tohu v-bohu*, or formlessness and void. Both are important to the truth of being made in the image of the Creator who is past all knowledge and description, who defies—and includes—opposites. In the path of healing, everything is included.

The sephirot—the Attributes of God described in the diagram of the Tree of Life, or Etz Chaim—have been described as the inner structure of Reality, as intermediaries between the limitlessness of God and the limited life of humanity. But what does this really mean? Are they found only in some abstract, conceptual, or mental space? Are they esoteric models of Reality, the understanding of which is reached only through constant prayer and holiness? Do these sephirot have anything to do with our daily life? Are they present at breakfast or only at special seasons and special meals? Where is the connection between our world and these metaphysical concepts? Are they important only in the pursuit of holiness, or are they equally important in the pursuit of daily life? In being married or single? In looking at nature? In thinking about death?

When we begin to think about the sephirot, we soon enter a world of psychological symbolism, where the sephirot are symbols of something that is going on between Heaven and Earth. But for most of us, there is no feeling of immediacy, excitement, or presence. Instead, the sephirot are something we "learn about." Most descriptions of the sephirot have actually sent us in the wrong direction, away from what they really are.

To understand the sephirot is to reestablish the true connection between God and ourselves, a connection we often believe has been rent asunder, but which really still exists intact within every moment and every breath. Perhaps if we start from the beginning, these things now called sephirot can begin to make sense.

SEPHIROT: FROM REALITY TO SYMBOL

Before there were sephirot, there were sephirot, but they were not called that. We do not know what they were called, but people whose vision became unclouded through the constant search for God began to see and understand that the three dimensions of human life were not enough to take in the whole of human feeling and thinking. In only three dimensions, human life is meaningless: we are born without participating in the decision to be born and we die without assenting to that ending. How could this be reconciled with the notion that the universe, and by implication God, is just? Our very is-ness is a mystery. How did consciousness come about? How did we find ourselves here? Why are we here?

Yet in between these poles of the awesome fact of existence itself and the difficulties of living, there were those who found moments of illumination, when the sheer rightness of life was palpable. At those moments, all of life and death felt right. And these moments went well beyond the small concept of knowing *something*. They were about wisdom, which is often silent but knows and cannot be expressed in the usual manner. They were about Light, which was felt to emanate from the body and not just fall upon the body from the outside.

The palpable sense of the rightness of life was there when Moses gazed upon the everlasting fire in a bush that burned but was not consumed. It was with Daniel and Ezekiel as well. It was with Buddha when he awoke and saw the Morning Star. At those moments, our early ancestors probably felt themselves—as we do now—as limited and small creatures, and the Mystery of the Beyond as large. And yet the smaller and the larger seemed to fit together. There was no contradiction in that state of Light.

We need to look at this fulcrum point between the limited and the Absolute in order to understand the sephirot before they had the name sephirot, before there was a system to which they belonged. Our looking is like going to the well to understand the mystery of water; we need to understand the *that* that the sephirot are meant to represent and mediate. When we look in this way, we can reexperience what the explorers of the past experienced and make it live again firsthand; we can be in relationship to God once again, rather than thinking about a relationship that is yet to be real.

We know about the feeling of unification, of feeling at home in our world, because there have been others who have spoken about this state of being. What does the *tzaddik,* or righteous sage, know that we do not know? When the tzaddik says, "It is God's will. It is God's way," we somehow believe him. There is something innate in the character of the person that makes us respond to him as a lineage-holder of truth, someone to whom we should pay attention. There is something reconciled within him, something whole and at ease.

Perhaps we have briefly experienced this God-connected state ourselves. But when we are not in this state of unification, we long for it. When it is gone, we have the human need to remember it. In fact, what most people call "happiness" is really a devolved notion of this unified state. We need to bring it back, and so we make a *sign* for it. Many systems have been invented to describe this *thing* before which language falls silent; many symbols have been made to *stand for* what words cannot express.

Kabbalistically speaking, this is the realm of Yetzirah, the world of symbols and signs, the place where reality is still looked upon secondhand, reflectively. There is no direct contact with Divinity in Yetzirah when it is separated from the other universes. There is only contact by proxy, which is to say indirect contact through memory. Then we settle for substitutes, *symbolic* representations of the real thing. We are simply strict when we could be holy; we are preachy when we could be vulnerable; we are lonely when we could be Alone.

Signs are useful, but only insofar as they point the direction. When we start confusing the sign for the Holland Tunnel with the tunnel itself, we are in trouble! Signs are not real things; they hold nothing within themselves and are nothing. They are fingers pointing in a direction, important only in that they are *used* to find the way. Unless you know the living magic of the ancient Egyptian hieroglyphs, they are simply parts of ancient ruins. Yoga on paper gains no results. Prayers conceived of but not spoken are mute messengers who have lost their memory. Unless you know how to experience the sephirot as conditions, they remain a series of curiosities, helping us pass away the time while we *think* about God, but never finding a way of inviting God into our heart.

On the other hand, our ability to remember God through signs is a God-given gift in and of itself. These signs—products of our thinking process—are often our best way of finding which direction to go. Signs allow us to form communities of seekers, to find like-minded people with whom to develop a culture based on love of the Eternal. Finally, signs and symbols allow us to create a path wherein we can do the work of the personality, turning the soil as it were, for the seeds only God can plant.

Yet signs and symbols need to die in order for us to experience Reality, to meet that portion of God we can understand. For many, the thought of God without the experience of God is unbearable. There is no substitute for tasting; not even a brilliantly written description will do. Even when we find the well, the water is in the drinking.

FROM SYMBOL TO REALITY

While we are in Yetzirah-only consciousness, we cannot truly experience what the sephirot are—that is, what the name sephirot represents: a real and living quality. To say that the sephirot are Attributes or illuminations does us little good. What the sephirot really are—dualities that are in love with the Absolute, holders of relational space—needs to enter our body for us to understand their immediacy. We then can also understand the consequences of joining with them and thereby facing God.

As human beings, we are creations whose essence (and conflict) is such that we have a personal self and yet want to be part of the larger reality called God. This "person" has the attribute of standing apart, of looking from some invisible vantage point without that vantage point being named, indicated, or even noticed. In other words, the personal is *always* in relationship to something, but the way personal beings feel this and express it is usually from what Martin Buber called the I-It position: neither of the pair is fully realized or alive. Instead, they both are symbolic of something that is kept at arm's length and not lived fully. In other words, in the I-It stance, we are not in true relationship to a thing we confront face-to-face, but in relationship to a *symbol* that stands for the thing-in-itself.

Buber says that when we are in the I-It paradigm, we *experience* the relationship rather than—in my words—*partake innocently* of it. We are then involved in commentary upon the relationship, rather than in the relationship itself. We are feeling ourselves feeling instead of being in the moment. So it is with the sephirot. Most of the words written about the sephirot have been from the perspective of Yetzirah-only: they were the *symbols* (or *became* the symbols) that great thinkers came up with in order to try to transmit the living experience of the Two-in-One, the finite in the Infinite, the individual held in the Heart of God.

Direct experience of conscious relationship, however, happens only in Briah. While through God's mercy the level of integration that is called Briah can be reached through Assiyah or Yetzirah, the living God becomes a presence in our hearts only at the briatic level of unification, whether it be through assiyatic "actions" accomplished with kavannah—which reach briatic conclusions—or yetziratic "feelings" that achieve the same openness and luminosity.

The sephirot are not things, nor do they point to things. Instead, they are a continuum of Unity and the experiences of Wholeness. Because they are nondual, when we study them properly, we are transformed. They are not separate from the conditions of our lives. They are not outside our lives—our lives are within them. We are the sephirot and the sephirot are us. This is the final study; all other studies lead to this one: actually becoming awake to our already established connection to God. So an interesting question is: What does the Tree of Life look like from the level of Unity? What is a sephira when it is a living experience and not a symbolic or remembered one?

In the *Sefer ha-Yetzirah,* one of the oldest extant kabbalistic texts, the first verse ends with these words: "And He created His universe with three books: with text, with number, and with telling." This is an important statement. It is asserting that three modes of creating were used to make our universe and that these modes are all somewhat different, though they emanate from the same Source. In effect, the *Sefer ha-Yetzirah* is saying that *all* created or manifested things have these three qualities within them. This would, of course, include the sephirot, which stand at the border between the manifest and unmanifest world.

To understand the Tree of Life, we need to understand the essential qualities of "text," "number," and "telling." For reasons that will become apparent later, I will address these three modalities slightly out of order, beginning with number.

Number

We learn number first, directly from the body. And through the body, which is our vehicle for living in the world, we learn the "number-ness" of the outer world as well. Numbers are specific and essential. The more we notice the world, the more numerical it seems. Right below the surface of things the world seems to be filled with *counting*. We notice the four seasons and the hours of the day and night: the passage of time is written in the book of our body. The Torah's first book—Genesis—details the division of the indivisible plenum into separate things that make the world a useful place for separate beings: Heaven *and* Earth, light *and* darkness, day *and* night, earth *and* water.

Through the medium of counting, we can abstract the world and generalize its rules. We can numerically define the spirals in shells and pinecones; the waves in sand, oceans, and galaxies; the vortices in streams; and the whorls in eyes and ears. They are all formed in the image of number. Through limits, specificity, quantity, and their inter-relationships, we can make a world. From this point of view, number is intimately tied up with consciousness.

Number—which allows for the world of addition, subtraction, multiplication, division, geometric shapes, identities, and differences—allows us to build the human world from God's hidden mathematical laws. The pyramids were built through the vehicle of number. The creation of the implements of worship is described in Exodus in numerical terms as well.

Through number we can see beneath the surface of the world. Number's depth is not interior in the sense of psychology, but descriptive. It is dispassionate and clear, and plays—sometimes invisibly—on the surface of things. Number is above all scientific, concerned with the stuff the world is made of, where it came from and where it is going.

In one of the most potent kabbalistic descriptions of the Creation process, the Divinity first withdraws its essence to leave a vacated space where God is not, so that individual beings—no longer nullified in God's greater Light—can exist. This withdrawal, or contraction, is called the *tzimtzum*. With the tzimtzum comes the advent of separate beings who need to make sense of the world, and number is one of the ways this need is transformed into knowing.

The *Sefer ha-Yetzirah* is saying that one of the basic creative principles is the ability to delineate and separate: to find the useful, generalized patterns in the midst of the natural world. This principle of creative delineation can also be seen as a way of describing what the ego's job is in our own, personal psyches. The philosopher Anton Ehrenzweig called this job *articulating consciousness*. Above all, the ego is interested in usefulness. It wants to make, to create, to find, to explore, to query, to understand, to discover, and to discover again.

Here I am equating the alert form of consciousness with ego. This type of consciousness—only one of many possible types of consciousness—forms around the "seed" of the ego, which is the essential "actor" of the separate self. The ego is the strange attractor of so-called alert consciousness, bending and making reality form around its interested eye. Though it seems to deal directly with the world, the ego is the great abstractor of the world. It separates itself from the world in an effort to control and make sense of it. The ego is life's great filmmaker.

This type of consciousness is concerned with reducing reality into pieces. Consciousness, from this perspective, is concerned with purity, seeing *this* as opposed to *that*. It picks out of the plenum that which is recognizable to it. It is the chooser, the delineator of foreground and background, and the progenitor of separateness. It is also closely allied with the senses, which are our doorways to the world of three dimensions. It seems proper then that one of the three creative modalities is number; this world is, after all, the world of separateness, and the ego and its attendant concerns, such as free will, doing, and physicality, require this type of consciousness above all. When we look at number, we are looking at something that makes sense to egoic consciousness, at something that presents a clear division between foreground and background, between *here* and *there*, between *something* and *nothing*.

Number gives us the binary world; there is a "one" or a "zero." It is highly useful, but ultimately it only mimics or skillfully points to the dynamic, flowing wholeness that is the Real World.

It is easy for our conscious mind to understand the origin of number. Somehow the very basis of existence is associated in our mind with number and quantity, which, though abstract, seem real to the touch. But why should number exist? That we do not ask that question points to the basic comfort we have with the existence of number. If I asked someone if number preexisted human beings, I think the answer would be yes. We can understand and abstract number and see it as a universal quality that exists independently of human beings. It seems to belong to God more than it belongs to us. When we look into number, it feels as if we are looking into eternity. Through number or mathematics, Einstein felt he was peering into the mind of God.

Text

There are other features of the world and of our own psyches whose creative essence is not numerical; they do not seem to conform to that mode of being and representation. So it is not surprising that the second of the *Sefer ha-Yetzirah's* three necessary modalities for the Creation of the world—expressed as book, text, and word—has some important features that numbers do not have. But when we first try to understand the second modality, we run into a stumbling block. Book, text, and word are all a part of linguistics or language, and the concept of language itself seems to be an entirely human thing that has no existence without human beings. However, a deeper look reveals that when the world is examined through the route of language, new and profoundly important features begin to show themselves. This new lens sees new things. In fact, some intriguing genetic research has revealed that linguistic features are expressed structurally in the central piece of protein that is the blueprint for our physical being.

In 1994, several scientists from Harvard University, Boston's Beth Israel Hospital, and Boston University began to study what is commonly called "junk DNA." These are the larger, noncoding regions of the DNA sequences that do not—on the surface—have a clear-cut function. They also do not reveal any perceptible mathematical order. Drawing on the remarkable work of George Zipf and Claude Shannon—the first a "dynamic philologist" and the second one of the world's leading information theorists—the Boston investigators found that information was indeed being carried by these noncoding sequences, although the underlying structure was *linguistic* rather than mathematical—that is to say, the information was encoded in ways that became clear only when the researchers looked at linguistic patterns.

In the 1930s and 1940s, George Zipf began looking at languages and especially at how words statistically reappeared in texts. Among many other startling discoveries, he noticed that when words were ranked in frequency of use and then plotted on a double logarithmic graph, a specific pattern was produced. This pattern showed a distribution curve, from very frequently used words to very infrequently used words. Most interesting, this distribution curve was exactly the same for every language Zipf studied. It was also found to be present when other data were plotted, such as ranking cities by population or companies by income. Zipf later enunciated this logarithmic pattern as a mathematical formula now called Zipf's Law. This law is especially interesting because it shows a commonality between aspects of communication—the frequency with which we use words in common speech and writing—and the ordering of other types of information we would not normally associate with any form of linguistic pattern.

It had long been assumed that the important parts of DNA were the sequences often termed "coding areas." These are the portions of the molecule in which strings of amino acids form combinations of the eight base pairs. The rest of the DNA molecule was often disparaged as "junk DNA." It seemed to hold no particular pattern and was therefore ignored, since it did not seem to contain useful information. But when the Boston investigators plotted the amino acid sequences in the noncoding areas and applied Zipf's Law, they found that these areas of the chromosome conformed to the law, meaning that they contained linguistic information or a specific type of ordering also found in language.

These scientists also applied some of Claude Shannon's work in communication and information theory to the discovery of a pattern in the so-called junk portions of DNA. One of Shannon's concerns was how information such as computer data or, more specifically at the time he was working, telephone conversations, vie with "noise"—which is in essence a kind of information that we do not want, which degrades the conversation we want to hear. Shannon's aim, while having important theoretical implications, was also quite practical: he wanted to be able to suggest ways to design circuits that would make the telephone system more reliable, that would increase the ability of information to win the fight with noise.

One of the concepts he studied was *redundancy* in language. He discovered that in all natural languages the redundancy factor is above zero, which means that information can be successfully communicated even if there is damage to a section of a "message." The scientists working on DNA found that the redundancy factor of the noncoding areas was *also* not zero. This means that, just like in a natural language, the noncoding areas were obeying laws that had to do with linguistic communication as opposed to mathematical law.

In the case of the coding areas of DNA, a simple mistake in one pair can alter the entire expression of a gene; small changes lead to chaotic conclusions. But the noncoding areas allow the continued transmission of information despite possible missing amino acids and other mistakes, thus constraining chaos. How the coding and noncoding areas of DNA work together to express our biological nature still remains to be discovered.

As a final test of the linguistic properties of DNA, these scientists did one more remarkable thing: they assigned colors of the spectrum to both the coded and the noncoded portions of the DNA and produced pictures of what the colors looked like when sequenced in this manner. The coded portions produced a hodgepodge of color in no discernable sequence, whereas the noncoded areas produced a perfectly flowing spectrum, from red all the way to blue.

I am deeply touched by the fact that human beings carry within them, at the deepest cellular level, both numerical information (as in the coded portions of DNA) and linguistic information (as in the remaining, much larger, portions of cellular DNA). These linguistic features of our DNA not only predate human language; they are included in the basic makeup of our bodies, minds, and spirits.

If number defines physical space, then the space of word, text, and book might be best called *linguistic* space. Linguistic space is a manifestation of an organizational process that follows an invisible strange attractor, expressing a different level of relationship, one that is not number-based, not binary, and more capable of describing other aspects of Reality that number can only hint at. The search for God must lead us out of the limited world of the exact into the larger paradigm of the Real, which includes all things, exact or not. (From this perspective, even *number* must eventually yield its seeming exactness to reveal its metaphoric and linguistic heart.) A close look at the linguistic features of human language may give us additional insights into God's Speech.

One of the differences between linguistic space and geometric space is that it possesses the qualities of rhythm and redundancy. Linguistic rhythm is not a regular beat or uniform pattern, but rather closer to the idea of *pulse*. A totally even or regular beat is not life enhancing, whether in the heart or in music, dance, painting, poetry, or any other art. In linguistic terms, rhythm means something more like the irregular stress on certain syllables in speech; or the accents and pronunciations that change with the context of what is being said; or slang, idiom, alliteration, assonance, and echoes—all of which condense meaning into both more economical, space-saving turns of phrase and yet more profound and subtle levels of information. This quality is the curve of poetry that is recognized as a living thing in any language where it is found.

The human mind and heart delight in pitting the regular against the irregular: stresses and strains against the even, the curving path against the straight line. This rhythm is uneven and eventful, many layered and changeable. It has an impact upon our bodies and minds that is profoundly below the level of thought and even feeling, though it evokes both of these. Linguistic rhythm is another way of dividing up the plenum, leading to new dimensions and consequences not found in the world of number.

Redundancy in language—and here I am talking about the language *beneath* language, the language that predates the invention of the various human tongues—is primarily a way of communicating. We can call this language *metalanguage*. Kabbalah teaches us that this metalanguage existed before there were beings to speak to each other. It is a form of consciousness that exists in every piece of created matter or energy.

From the kabbalistic perspective, when we look at why this metalanguage exists, we might say that it is the modality that addresses itself to the concept of *touching,* how one thing—which is separate from all other things—can touch something else. It is about joining, and is the universal quality that lies beneath all communication, which is actually a form of *touching*. Redundancy in language is simply a way of making sure this touching can best happen.

Hence, this metalanguage is—on the personal level—about psychology, or the inner, spaceless space that makes up the human mind. On the interpersonal level it is about the possibility of community, which results from many different people "touching" each other in some manner. Linguistic space is therefore not dimensional in the same way number is; it does not describe dimension, nor does it exist in time and space in the same way. It exists in informational or nondimensional space.

Linguistic space is as much about accident as it is perfection; it needs "noise" or the unclear, foreground *and* background, in order to be as clear as possible. In information theory, this additional noise-that-clarifies is called *stochastic resonance*. Linguistic space—because it is the Wholeness beneath appearances—unites several types of opposites, and uses those opposites to make resilient and economical communication. This metalanguage brings resiliency into the world. We can also call this resiliency *forgiveness;* it makes possible the manifestation of another one of God's laws of creation: Mercy.

Linguistic space is robust, unlike number, which is quantity-critical.

The natural and human worlds are filled with groupings of various things that need great robustness to continue to exist together. For example, a machine does not have great robustness: a gear missing a tooth, or a pump that does not work, will cause the machine—sooner or later—to fail. On the other hand, a human body or an ecosystem can endure many different types of stresses before it is irreparably damaged. Linguistic space says, in effect, "I will accept *degrees* of perfection. While the most perfect thing would *seem* to be best, I can make do with something less than perfect; I can extrapolate what I need. My wholeness can endure with something less than perfect. I can use imperfection to make a whole that is dynamic and flowing. My fundamental nature is not about perfection." This resiliency—which is a form of redundancy—is the living quality of forgiveness at work.

Because of its forgiving nature and its essence of touching, linguistic space allows room for the organic growth that number can only describe. This growth—which always involves opposites manifesting together—invites laughter and sorrow into the world. Growth always entails something being born and something dying, movement from one thing to another, unequal and dynamic conditions. The two together hide a third thing, which is the life principle itself.

Built around this seed, awareness forms the type of consciousness we call the "unconscious." While number is exact, word is not, and from it an entirely different world can grow. It is no accident that the first conscious foray into exploring the unconscious was made through art, wordplay, dreams, and other linguistic techniques. Human psychology is understood from the point of view of word, text, and book best of all, since it is modeled after the preexisting template of what we might call Divine Letters.

Our language—which is the human expression of our search for touching—is filled with a *vagueness* that makes touching possible. A vague word is one that includes borderline or inexact members in the set of meanings of that word. An example is *tall,* a borderline word I used as an example earlier. How "tall" is tall? We all know when we see a tall man or woman, but when we try to define exactly when "tall" starts and stops, we have no luck. The same is true of the word *red:* it is defined by what it is not. In the same way we could ask, "How far away is far?" It is only close to or distant from *near,* having no absolute meaning on its own, only a relational one.

Our language and everyday life are filled with vague words and vague concepts, yet we all understand each other. Why is this so? Mathematical consciousness would say that we simply haven't defined our terms well enough yet, that the answers will get clearer as we have more powerful thinkers with more powerful tools to break up Reality into smaller and smaller pieces until the problem is solved.

Yet, all of these *vague* words bring a certain feeling to life, and if we examine that feeling closely, we find that the realm of art is full of vagueness, whether it is manifested art like music and painting or the inner sense of art, the attraction we all feel toward rhythm and beauty and humor. Vagueness seems to imbue life with some type of meaning that can be talked about only in a vague way. A mathematical analysis of a work of Picasso's or a symphony of Mahler's would betray the very purpose of their art.

The philosopher R. M. Sainsbury defines *vagueness* as a "boundaryless concept." He uses the example of the color spectrum: "I believe, by contemplating a very familiar case [that is] the color spectrum, as displayed, for example, in an illustration in a book on color, looking carefully, we can discern no boundaries between the different colors. They stand out as clearly different, yet there are no sharp divisions. There are bands, but not bounds." Sainsbury goes on to say in the same essay that "boundaryless concepts tend to come in systems of contraries: opposed pairs like child/adult, hot/cold, weak/strong, true/false. . . . This is a natural consequence of boundarylessness." Seen another way, to understand the wholeness of a boundaryless word we look at what a thing is being compared to in order to understand the concept at hand.

This reveals that the unitive principle, when made manifest in the dualistic world, always—like the simultaneous wave and particle nature of light—appears in the form of a bifurcated manifestation. In other words, Unity appears as a pair of opposites. Another way to say this is that so-called opposites really hide a deeper layer of Wholeness beneath or within their appearance—if we only know how to see. Linguistic space is similarly continuous and not discrete. It is therefore an expression of the plenum and not a description of it. Because linguistic space can exist in vagueness, without having to make a choice for "only this" or "only that," it is seamlessness itself.

Originally, there were no separate symbols for numbers, and letters were assigned numerical values. So numerical consciousness and linguistic consciousness were unified in a way that is not available to the modern mind. The kabbalistic methodology of gematria works—that is, sees into the underlying level of Unity in creation—*not* because the Hebrew language has a mathematical basis, but because it has a *numerolinguistic* basis. Wholeness, too, has both a mathematical and a linguistic basis. So it is to be in the service of God. We cannot serve by simply following *number*—that is, the rules or commandments. Our service must include the dimension that unifies our separate lives and the life of God for our connection to be Real. So must we understand the sephirot: from both the heart and the mind, and not from one or the other.

Telling

The final modality the *Sefer ha-Yetzirah* discusses is telling, and this may be the most important of all. This telling, which is communication, is how the modalities of number/quantity and word/quality are made manifest. The two sides of the human brain each deal with one of these modalities, and we have an articulate mouth in the middle; this is no accident. Telling is an interactive mode that defines *relational space*, which is the combined product of number and word *in action*. Telling, or narrative, brings us out of higher-level space into the world of duality. To *tell* we need a speaker and a listener; we need distance to *tell* over and *difference* to *tell* between.

The holographic picture of each sephira, each one a container for an entirely new Tree, ad infinitum, is the *sefer*—meaning "book" or narrative—of the True Self, the One who is connected. To truly feel the power of the sephirot, we must enter the narrative, the telling, and be swept away by the rhythm that underlies all of existence.

Entering the narrative is to avoid all symbolism through the power of engagement, and to deal with the thing-in-itself in every way possible, *including* interpretation and symbolism. To be with the sephirot, or Attributes, is to be in the incredibly rich assonance of a kind of living poetry. We are transformed by reading. We are changed by the listening, no longer alone, but utterly changed. In the state of change, we are no longer separate from the narrative, but are aware of the underlying rhythm of creation, alive to life.

For me, the mathematical consciousness and egoic mind point to the underlying Wholeness; they describe this "thing of importance," which is why mathematicians are entranced by the beauty of certain equations. But the metalinguistic unconscious—which in my explanation includes the conscious portion of the mind—is its direct expression. It is Beauty itself, silent and unspoken.

Number *points* to this Beauty, but only the combination of number and word lets Beauty emerge and speak. In God's Reality, number and word are intimately bound together. In these numero-linguistic spaces, "two" is a different world than "one," and not simply the additive quantity. Even when "one" and "one" are added together, the new level reached is *qualitatively* different. We call this difference "two." From this perspective, numerical equations are the movements not only of quantities, but also of *qualitative* differences. Even in gematria, it is a mistake to think of numerically equivalent words as linguistically equivalent. They may spring from the same origin, the same underlying *meta-concept*, but they are not equivalents in any way. Rather, they express different dimensions of relationship, different facets of the Real.

Because it contains both number and word, the Tree of Life is a completely robust system in which our participation is key to its unfoldment and our unfolding. It is *our* Kingdom, *our* Foundation, *our* Victory, and *our* Splendor, and it is all around us. If we maintain our separateness, our intellectual distance, we can never know what the sephirot are. To understand the great impersonal aspect of God, we need to make it all personal first, through telling, which is the great *touching* we must do with Life.

This is why we chant and sing our praises out loud—not just because it gives us pleasure, but because it changes us by virtue of recognizing the story we are: the words *and* the flavor, the specifics of the prayer *and* the way the prayer *touches* the speaker as we listen. We cease for those moments being simply reflections of ourselves and become who we truly are.

APPLICATION TO INTEGRATED KABBALISTIC HEALING

Telling—or the nondual narrative and listening—is of utmost importance in the practice of Integrated Kabbalistic Healing. In A Society of Souls community, we consider our diagnostic process an important part of the healing and not just a preliminary to the main event. In it, we apply our understanding that the sephirot are related to both number and word, as holders of specific qualities from the egoic and alert consciousness point of view, and as mysteries into which we must descend and remain in order to emerge with understanding. We recognize that—being made in the image of God—we are numerical *and* linguistic beings. Being with the client in this exquisite fashion lets an intimacy exist that is in itself a healing event. Since we are attempting to work in a nondual milieu, this intimacy is never invasive or overbearing, but filled with Presence, which is to say filled with the intimate One.

Deeply involved in linguistic space, we are also joined with number, which allows us to make use of the specific, the technical, and the egoic consciousness. Nothing is left out. We understand that the Tree of Life is a combination of essences and conversations, and that the narrative pictured there is the story of our lives and the lives of everything that is.

In Integrated Kabbalistic Healing, the diagnostic process—the special form of listening that is the *telling* of the moment—takes place when the healer listens to why the client has come to him or her in this special way that encompasses both the world of number and of word.

This artistic process is counterintuitive. Unlike other diagnostic schema, it does not seek to narrow down which of the many possible kabbalistic healings the client should receive for his or her problem.

The diagnostic process is a *complexifying* process, the opposite of characterologies that reduce the suffering one to mere number, mere idea. Instead, with utter trust in the holographic nature of God, we understand that the problem that brought the client to us—whether it was understood by the client to be physical, emotional, or spiritual—is holographically spread throughout that person's life, alongside its cure. As the old Zen saying goes, "Illness makes its own medicine."

In the diagnostic process, the healer does not seek out clarity at the expense of confusion; does not seek answers only to lose the questions; does not see the client's problems, whether physical, emotional, or spiritual, as captured or fixed in one portion of the Tree of Life as a mechanical construct. Rather, the healer sees how the client's discontinuity, his or her *human suffering*, particularizes throughout the Tree in subtle and varied manners, affecting its growth, its dimensional relationships, and, finally, its manifestations in physical, emotional, and spiritual life. The process reveals both the healing that is needed for that client at that moment *and* an intimate understanding of the humanness of the client, who has, through various means, successful and unsuccessful, always been searching for Wholeness.

In a sense, the diagnostic process is a falling into truth rather than a rising above to gain an overview. It understands that the view from the bottom will show us the view from the top, that the way to the highest is from where we are, is actually *within* where we are. Using clarity *and* confusion, specific knowledge *and* floating in the unknown, hierarchical *and* holographic thinking, the heart *and* the mind, the healer emerges from the process with the exact healing that will help that client at that time.

In this process, the healer does not stand apart: the truth of each sephira can be known only as the body becomes the ground of being in which the consciousness of each sephirot is palpably experienced. Students doing the work of Integrated Kabbalistic Healing do enormous work clearing their instruments to be able to safely feel this at-one-ment. Since the body was our first line of defense against the pain of living, it must be reclaimed as a safe port in every storm. To be present, fully three-dimensional in a three-dimensional world, is one of the hardest tasks the healer has to learn. Through many meditations, philosophical lectures, and practical applications, the student slowly learns to reenter the body-as-vehicle, the body as truth. This is the body-mind-spirit who can find union with another.

And yet in this union there is no merging. Because number is as real as word and telling, we strive always to know where we are and who we are, behind all nonessential masks and secondhand concepts.

So we as healers become readers of words and numbers, sentences, paragraphs, chapters, and books. We strive to know the mathematics of the soul and its language as well. We look for psychological nuance, ear-rhythms, memorizations of the body, and hardnesses of the spirit. We look for cues, spirals, economy of phrasing, theme, leitmotif, and recurring song. We look for the mathematical descriptions—which are the still pictures of a fleeting world—and participate in the intimate, flowing movement that is beyond experience. We seek out the primal life energy, remembering always that even this only points to something yet greater, the One who made it all, the One whose purpose we are.

Healing, then, takes place because the specific is married to the vague, the changeable to the constant, Heaven to Earth. This is the truth of our being and, being in that truth, we heal. The language before language allows us entry into the world of the unmanifest, and number gives us the key to what has been made ready by word.

"In our beginning is our end; in our end, our beginning." So says the *Sefer ha-Yetzirah*. We are made of the permutations of the letters of Reality; calcium in one form holds up the body with bones; calcium ions in the brain make memory possible.

The Torah could not be written only as a series of laws, as a series of codes. The code of the Ten Commandments needed the story that surrounds it because, like coded DNA, it needs a context in which to build the body of Life. The Etz Chaim, or Tree of Life, is the story of this story, the enfolded outline of what, once it is unfolded, will turn out to be the story of our lives. The sephirot can be understood only by the act of changing from someone who sits outside the sephirot to someone who is *inside* and *outside* simultaneously, who can think about the sephirot and realize that *he or she is being thought by them* at the same time.

This is not Eros, where we are completely entranced and absorbed by the Beloved with no thought of ourselves. Rather, this is marriage, where we are separate *and* together, always alone and always mated. It is the state of Duality in Oneness, Oneness in Duality.

The sephirot are the songs that God sings. The Tree itself is our self: sung to, sung by, spoken of, and speaking. We are part of the vocabulary of the universe, the ancient vocabulary that includes both number and place, content and context. And searching for ourselves is useless: we *are* the song we are looking for.

In this state of consciousness, when I look at the world, I see God speaking. Each tree is a sentence; the flow of hillside and water, the roads, cars, people, animals, books, and the dry leaves of autumn are all the manifestation of the living Law. I watch how the cooling air curls above the pond, how everything interacts to form this vast, unending sentence that is the world and could be Heaven, the ongoing utterance of God.

QUESTIONS AND ANSWERS

Question: How can the sephirot be used to lead a better life, to awaken to the Divine?

Jason: As represented by the sephirot, the indefinable quality of the world has its basis in the metalinguistic *and* numerical impulses. When both are working together, the essential-exact and the essential-inexact make the self-organizing and holographic features of the world possible. In purely human terms, these qualities make it possible for human beings to awaken to the Reality of God. Without them, this awakening would not be possible.

Having ten sephirot—each not only holographically containing all the others, but also having number integrated with qualitative differences and not just quantitative ones—makes the system of the Tree of Life redundant and resilient, less liable to error or mistake.

The holographic principle says in effect: While it is true that tremendous effort is needed in order to make progress in spiritual work, it is also true that Reality is not only linear; the way to God is not only over there, a long way off. Instead, because God is everywhere, God is simultaneously in every particle of Reality. Each piece of manifestation is God made. Human beings may do something else with creation, but God's holiness is embedded in each and every thing. So God is never far off. God is Here.

The self-organizing principle, when applied theologically, says, "While it is true that we have brains and hearts that guide us and are the main centers of our thoughts and feelings, it is also true that every piece of reality is endowed with Divinity. This God-seed-in-each-thing can be trusted. When we set up the right conditions of faith and practice, hard work and easy acceptance, we allow this Intelligence to emerge. Then each piece knows where it is going and what it is making. The ego knows, the head knows, the heart and body know. Communication does not have to be established; it was already there, in the very structures themselves, in what went into making the structures manifest in that way. We are made in the image of God, in every piece and nerve."

While in traditional Lurianic Kabbalah, the state of *nekudim,* or "points," is seen as a nonrelational state in which giving *and* receiving is not possible, from my perspective the *nekudic* state is an important developmental stage whereby each "piece" of matter, energy, or consciousness is fully infused with self-organizing Intelligence or its essential connection to God. *Nekudic consciousness* is a condition of total self-responsibility, which is an essential quality for deep spiritual work.

In fact, unless this Intelligence becomes individuated, the integrated state of giving and receiving, called *berudim,* could not happen. If these so-called points or fragments were not individualized, with self-existence—which is the same as self-responsibility—they would slip back into the state of enfoldment called *akudim,* where all intelligence is *bound.* Only individuals, using their full individual free will, can return to God fully. And when they do so, it is as something new and not as a return to an earlier, oceanic, infantile state of being. Our wish for the "golden age" of childhood should not be confused with Heaven.

In self-organizing environments, where each member is totally and individually responsible, there is no centralized ego; each part responds personally to the Whole, and the flow of life is then evenly distributed to, and arises equally from, all quarters. This consciousness is nondual, connecting God and us in a seamless Whole. All levels of creation become responsible to the Ultimate Life Principle. This is the opposite of an indirect, hierarchical arrangement; here each individual becomes a "light unto himself," a necessary condition for joining the community of God. Then each person, like each sephira, is fully individualized, a *nekudic* individual holding a portion of the Infinite, standing in the Light ready to join and touch.

It Starts with a Disappointment . . .

. . . and It Ends in Light

It starts with a disappointment that is so completely shocking that the wave it makes as it lands continues to the present day. We land on Earth created in an exquisite manner, our eyes ready to look, to be so completely touched and touching that light, skin, air, and earth are the same thing. We cannot believe that things have fallen apart so quickly, and we find ourselves with no words to grasp this reality, so it becomes ungraspable, and strangles us just when we were expecting great things.

IT STARTS WITH A DISAPPOINTMENT . . .

AT FIRST WE DO NOT KNOW what is going on. We don't know whom to blame. Things are simply wrong, and we ratchet down our expectations into a movie about the real thing, or maybe the screen goes blank entirely and we live another life.

We are shocked beyond one belief and into another: that the world is not right and that we will have to make our way as best we can; that we will have to give up our galaxy for a room that is fed by corners, that is all angles and walls and in-betweens.

So we invent time and space and continue, and we lick our mother's cheek and smile.

This is the beginning of the birth of the great loneliness, the origin of the one who takes all of our faces and wears them like masks and stares back at us through puzzled eyes, a confusion within the lens of things and intricate distances we do not know how to transverse. There is only one hope: that we can climb the tree of our lives once again, reliving our original fall, and willingly jump into the place that was supposed to have been home.

Why do we have a so-called self, a kind of consciousness that looks at itself over and over again? And isn't this self really a continuum of many different types of selves, from ones that hang carelessly on the wall, used when needed, to ones we obsessively wear, to ones that we cannot get rid of, that stick to our skins like rubber or freeze our skins like frost?

There is a divine reason that the self of self-looking was created; it was neither an accident nor a mistake. But very few of us ever get to see the real version of this self-that-looks and instead battle daily with the self that is separated from the Whole by pain and longing, the self that is supposed to be remedied by quests and imagination.

Each of these selves takes the original individual self and lays over it yet another version. Each of these versions is created by another type of difficulty, ones we pass down through generations to each other like some dark torch in a relay race of despair.

The path back from each of these versions of the original individual self is somewhat different. On one path we need to stand alone; on another we need to join with others; for yet another we need to be brave; for another we need to tremble and shake. For some, we need water with its flow and coolness. For others, we need fire that can burn us up.

Most of us need several journeys to trace our way back to our original individual face, the face that can exist only in duality the way duality exists as part of Wholeness Itself.

The particular small self, this particular difficulty, is the one that was created by disappointment. It is one of the most difficult to cure because the disappointment that created it happened so early and so quickly. This self was created in a moment of lightning and was followed by years of rain falling on dead land, land without a covering of soil, without fragrance or feel.

But because in reality we are *not* this land, because we are something much greater—even though it is hidden beneath thick layers of rock—the very barrenness of the land is our salvation. The pain we feel at the unproductiveness of life eventually burns through the rock like a universal solvent, and we touch, if we are willing, the bedrock of our own soul, which lies there, strangely protected in that dry and unwilling place.

We are walking down the street but we are in a movie; every move we make we see from the outside. We think, "It might rain soon," and we hear ourselves say it with a turn of phrase we hope will be historical when the history of our lives is read, long after we are dead, of course. Dead, but fondly remembered.

We look at other people and wonder if they are looking at us and what they think about us. We feel great power within us as well as creativity; we accomplish things but never feel really satisfied. We have sex in a mirror with a reversed woman or man: we enter someone else to get *outside* ourselves instead of *inside*.

We long to lead and are given positions of leadership, but then they fall apart, as if we cannot breathe and walk at the same time and need to stop. Someone else who is less worthy gets the post.

If we get too much attention, we close up. If we get too little, we wither. The moments when things are "just right" are quick and difficult to grasp. Although we feel sentimental and therefore apart, sometimes something gets through the wall of sentiment. Someone says, "Hi, sweetie!" or someone smiles with genuine warmth at seeing us, and we melt and want to give this person the world. This lasts until we become inexplicably angry, and that person becomes a demon for us, standing in the shadows, ignoring us; we believe—unconsciously—that this person probably hates us.

We go through life making connections—having sex, singing, being loved, and fearing being hated. We have no home really, and when we try to build one, we get confused: it doesn't look as much like home as some stranger's house we visited last week where we felt much more at home.

If we are determined and lucky—that is, strong, flexible, and in enough pain—and if our nerves have remained *alive* enough to feel this constant wail, we find ourselves having some continuous relationships, and though these relationships are often like fingernails on a blackboard that make us cringe, we know somewhere deep in our hearts that these connections are really like milk, and we sip slowly, knowing we would die without this nourishment.

We have some wisdom, it's true, but we have to give that up: we've made it into part of the movie. We have some understanding, but we have to abandon it for the rich fields of unknowing. We have a wandering spirit, but we have to give up that freedom to find the deeper freedom of making a place to live. We have to give up our belief in our own ignorance, because we *do* have wisdom and we *do* know. It often feels like we have no place to stand.

In a sense, we abandon the positions of every station and event on the Tree of Life and throw ourselves on the mercy of the Great Unknowable One: the One who makes the acid that will reduce our soul to nothing—or so we fear.

Someone listens to us.
Someone aids us.
Someone sings to us.
Someone puts up with us.
Someone sees our talents.
Someone likes us.
Someone does not place his or her own disappointment in us.
Someone understands our loneliness and is not afraid to face
it even though it means facing his or her own.

This person does not slip or falter, and because we now have a boon companion to go with us through the breathing in and out and the dry, mysterious places of Nothingness at the height and depth of breath, we begin to sink into our own lives. We eventually find out that this is the true life of God.

This is a journey of bearing pain and sorrow without blame. Of bringing home everything that belongs to us so that the God in us can reassemble it into a human being.

We go through many stages on the journey. There are moments of despair and triumph, moments of thinking we are done with the journey and moments of thinking we have never begun. Everything becomes confusing until finally we are confusion itself, and we find a strange calm in the middle of this storm. We go through apologizing for everything we have ever done. And we go through being our own man or woman: "Take us as we are or leave us alone."

Slowly, the drama departs. We are left small and frightened and we look in the mirror of our own hands and see what we have picked up along the road. It is not much. Our talents don't amount to much; at least, they don't save us. Our wisdom is laughable, vying between the greatest story ever told and unimaginable pettiness. We are occasionally kind and occasionally king, but nothing lasts.

We begin to walk with less expectation, lighter by the amputation of what might have been, what should have been, and what will be. It is then that we see the Great Disappointment.

We begin to understand that it starts with a disappointment that is so completely shocking that the wave it makes as it lands continues to the present day. We land on Earth created in an exquisite manner, our eyes ready to look, to be so completely *touched* and *touching* that light, skin, air, and earth are the same thing. We cannot believe that things have fallen apart so quickly and we have no words to grasp this reality, so it becomes ungraspable, and strangles us just when we were expecting great things.

We begin to see that *everyone* started out the same way, tender and hearted, bellied and trembling, excited and expecting only the best things, because we knew what God was: this glowing we felt within our heads and hands. There was no mistaking it.

Oh, these tenderhearted people! Such disappointment and longing!

And we begin to see that we might now know something else, something only grown-ups can know, something only someone who has been terribly disappointed can know, something someone knows only when he or she has gone through the fainting and the fire. It is this: within the disappointment are all of us. No one gets it right. And when we enter that disappointment, we enter the human race.

We hear the voice of God then, and it sounds like *touch* and *kiss*, and other people. We open to pain and open. And open to joy and open.

Then the masks fall away and we remain, looking at the day.

. . . AND IT ENDS IN LIGHT

The moment we look at the day we see that everything that is allowed to remain, remains in Light. Underneath every evil is the force that says, "This sadness should not be allowed to exist." Within every piece of split wood is the ax mark we made to tear ourselves apart, fearing for our sanity and our lives.

The universe is set up so that everything that we can be in the presence of, and remain whole with, returns from dust to diamonds, returns to its inherent Wholeness. When every pain, every separation, is allowed to remain—that is, to exist in the fullness of feeling—then the Light it is made of begins to emerge. It is the radiance of something freshly watered, the shine of what it is, which, of course, is God.

There is only One. There were never two. Bending, we look back at ourselves and see our wounded nature. Standing straight, sitting on the base of our own nature, we see not only what we were meant to be, but also what we really are: the prophet hiding in the cleft of rock and the back of the One who passes. The small face hidden behind hands, but peeping out through splayed fingers at the miracle of being, and the Ancient One who made fingers, and gave us the idea of looking itself.

We make a wind as we pass through life. Sometimes it is like a storm and sometimes like a breeze. Sometimes we float and sometimes we are torn. We are the tearing, the torn thing, and the wind that tears.

Everything ends in Light. It began that way, and all things, true to their Maker, continue and continue, following their deepest wish.

About A Society of Souls

In 1989, I began the journey that would lead to the creation of A Society of Souls, a school dedicated to the awakening of the human spirit through the work of Integrated Kabbalistic Healing, IM/personal Movement, and the Work of Return.

Now, ten years since the inception of the school, more than 350 people have graduated from its rigorous program. Perhaps several thousand more have been influenced, helped, and touched by the work these graduates have done in fields as varied as healing, law, teaching, psychiatry, psychotherapy, art, chiropractic, acupuncture, and other disciplines.

When I started the school, I looked for a name that would signal something about its intent and goal. I wanted to say that it would be about *souls* first of all, that we would try to deal with something eternal that we, as finite beings, contain in some way. I also wanted this to be *a* society of souls and not *the* society of souls, for I felt that the work we were going to do was basically the work of life, the work everyone who is living is given a chance to do. We might do it in a more concentrated way, a more chosen way, perhaps, but it would be the work of life.

My life has always, from my earliest memories, been involved with the questions of spirit. Why are we here? Where do we go? These were questions I remember thinking about at age four.

The school became my answer to these questions and my ongoing vehicle for exploring what is Real. The school has drawn intelligent, courageous, and dedicated students whose passion is the same as mine: to heal personally, to understand, to gain wisdom, and to awaken to God's presence.

When the school first started, I saw the work of Integrated Kabbalistic Healing (IKH) as being most useful for healers of all types. I had developed this work over a period of years from my understanding of the world of spirit, specifically Kabbalah.

As the years went by, my students taught me that the insights of IKH were applicable not only to the formal act of healing, but also to a level of insight that had implications for the way we live our lives.

Since acceptance to the school is by application and invitation, it has an interview process. During interviews I often ask potential students what relationship they have with failure. I tell them that I am not looking for newly minted healers or lawyers or teachers or therapists, but for people who have also failed, who have been knocked around by life. I do this because I am interested in people who have been disillusioned a bit, since what we are after is to be disillusioned entirely, so that we can see the Real in all its manifestations: the Real Self, Buddha-nature, God-realization, Submission—these are all names for the same "thing."

In founding the school, I was following another idea too: that *healing* and *awakening* should go together. Not only should they go together, but they should go together in a new way. My idea was not to feed enlightenment back into the spiritual pantry, but to *have a job as an enlightened being.* That job was healing, and healing could be done in myriad ways.

Some ASOS students have decided to become kabbalistic healers. Others use the work for self-healing. Still others modify the work, taking the insights into their own modality.

The study of Integrated Kabbalistic Healing takes four years of class work. In the IKH curriculum, we are really doing two things at once: studying the material and studying ourselves. IKH cannot be done without both; the work requires us to walk the walk and not just talk the walk.

In IKH we teach many of the healings I have created from my understanding of Kabbalah and the awakened state. Students learn the Healing of Immanence, the various sephirotic healings, and the advanced healings of the world of Briah, including the Healing of Threads, the Healing of Immanence in Briah, Morphic Healing, and the Healing of Certainty. We learn these healings not as abstract techniques, but rather in relationship to life.

Along with the healings, we teach the art form called the Diagnostic Process, which forms the core method of understanding and assessing our clients and their life situations in order to choose the appropriate kabbalistic healing for them. Unlike most diagnostic schemas, it is based on our ability to complexify, rather than reduce, our clients' symptoms in order to characterize them.

Our approach to Kabbalah is nondual. Our understanding of God is that God is Here. Our model of the universe is that it is present to do the work of relationship, and our understanding of ourselves is that when we are fully human—not fully perfect—we can know that we have been with God always. Our community supports this important work as tenderly as possible.

In the mid-1990s, I began working on the second pillar of work that goes into making up the teachings of A Society of Souls: IM/personal Movement.

In this movement work, consisting of two levels, IM/1 and IM/2, participants gain a deep and abiding, body-centered understanding of the unitive state, which, from the point of view of IM, is neither personal nor nonpersonal. The unitive state is the understanding of the origin place of both duality and the Absolute.

This movement work allows practitioners to learn to abide in the Absolute while living a fully human life that is in touch with the Divine.

The third tier of work, completed most recently, is the Work of Return. This work is about self-healing and is a powerful path for understanding the way the unintegrated ego creates illness on all levels of being. We see the effectiveness of this work not only in personal transformation, but in the management of chronic pain, working with post-traumatic stress, and ongoing spiritual exploration as well. It arose not only from my kabbalistic understanding but also through understanding the Buddhist concept of Emptiness or Boundlessness as expressed in the Prajnaparamita or Heart Sutra. The Work of Return is the manifestation of the Great Mother's kindness of heart.

A Society of Souls—these words still touch my heart. Over the last ten years, I have watched the community that has been formed grow more autonomous and strong. I have watched it welcome in people who are new to this study with great openheartedness. I have watched it grow in creativity as the teachings have penetrated into the nooks and crannies of the real world.

Readers who are interested in finding out more about this path of the body, mind, and heart are invited to visit us at our Web site: www.kabbalah.org. You can communicate with us through the site or by writing to us at A Society of Souls, 17 Witherspoon Court, Morristown, NJ 07960. You can also reach us by telephone: 908-538-7689.

Glossary

Adonai. The divine Name associated with Malchut. See also EHYE.

Amidah. "The Standing" (because the prayer is said standing), or "The Prayer." This is one of the central prayers of the Jewish daily ritual, traditionally recited three times each day. It is sometimes referred to as the *Shemoneh Esrei,* which means "Eighteen Benedictions," the number of sections it originally contained. It includes this statement of the origin and culmination of healing: "Heal us, O Lord—then we will be healed; save us and then we will be saved, You are our Praise . . . ," tying our personal and ultimate healing to the supreme Unity of God.

Assiyah. The name of the kabbalistic universe that is closest to our human realm. It is the world of action, habit, and behavior. It is in this realm that evil, or disconnection from God, is acted out most abundantly. The vehicle for change in this universe is our behavior, the actions we take and the choices we make in choosing actions that bring us closer to God, the Source of our True Self. In Assiyah, God's Light and consciousness is in its most concealed state since this universe cannot contain the level of freedom and relationship found in the other universes. See also Yetzirah, Briah, Atzilut.

Atzilut. The most essential, or most deeply integrated, of the kabbalistic universes. Atzilut is the universe that is most transparent to God's Light, having never been shattered during the first emanation of the sephirot. In other words, it is so integrated that it provides little barrier to the essential truth of God's world—hence, its nickname of "Nothingness." Atzilut is completely absorbed in the divine milieu. For human beings, there is some reason to believe that atzilutic consciousness makes itself known as the seeker understands the actions of Assiyah, the feelings of

Yetzirah, and the nonduality of Briah. Empowered with the knowledge of this journey, the seeker returns to daily life with other people, complete with its pain and joy. This new joining resurrects the original atzilutic unity of the world with Heaven, revealing the formerly hidden motivation of God in creating the world. For human beings, this is Atzilut itself. From the linear or hierarchical point of view, this universe is almost unreachable by our current possible level of purification. From the holographic point of view, however, it is not so much *reachable*—as the potential linear product of purification—as "possible to manifest" as a state of surrender and grace. When we go full circle in the spiritual journey, we find that God was never far from us, but rather closer than we could ever imagine. When our lives are fully filled with this completion, and when we begin to live this truth with other people—seeing them as they are, sharing and using our knowledge to bring our fellow beings to the root of their being and therefore into relationship with God—we might be said to be living an atzilutic life, the life of *healing* and *return*. See also Assiyah, Briah, Yetzirah.

Ayn-Sof. The kabbalistic term for God, meaning literally "Without End," or the "Ultimate Nothingness." This holy Name is considered the ultimate Name because it is beyond all conceptualization and compartmentalization. It is beyond manifestation and beyond nonmanifestation. It cannot be contained, defined, or limited in any way by the thinking mind. It differs from the Names of God in that these Names, such as Adonai, Elohim, Yah, and others, are the Names of God in the already created world.

Binah. The third sephira and the eighth gate. Binah—a feminine sephira—is translated as "Understanding."

Briah. The highly integrated universe of creation, which contains the consciousness of both Assiyah and Yetzirah. This universe stands at the interface of Oneness and separateness. It is the truth of our Oneness with the Creator and the truth of our individual existence and responsibility, the "oneness of Oneness and the Oneness of duality." This is the realm of "is-ness," wherein each thing—free of the objectification of Assiyah and the historical, psychological pain of Yetzirah—is finally completely itself and thus shines with the Light of God. While many people have touched pieces of the freedom that comes with the consciousness of this universe, Briah can also be approached as a kind of defense against the pain of living, a kind of dissociation for the purposes of protection against the difficulties of life. Embodied fully, however, Briah offers the chance to live a completely human life, with the suffering inherent in being a separate human being and the joy of knowing that we are, as each created thing is, part of God's creative activity. See also Assiyah, Atzilut, Yetzirah.

Chochmah. The second sephira and the ninth gate. It is translated primarily as "Wisdom."

EHYE. Each sephira, indeed each level of Reality, is associated with a divine Name. These divine Names are not symbolic of a level of Unity, but are holy expressions of that level itself. The Name EHYE is the Name associated with Keter, the first sephira and the one that is most purely transparent to the will and presence of the Creator. Its holiness requires that it is never pronounced directly. It is associated with the Attribute of pure Mercy, which contains no judgment at all. See also Adonai.

Etz Chaim. See Tree of Life.

Gevurah. The sixth gate and fifth sephira, feminine Gevurah is often translated as "Judgment," "Boundary," "Fire," "Severity," "Discipline," or "Awe." It is the complement to Hesed's endless openness.

Halacha. The Hebrew word for "the way," meaning "that path," or "the way to walk." Essentially, the Jewish path.

Hesed. The seventh gate and the fourth sephira. This masculine sephira is the condition or Attribute of "Loving-kindness" and the complement to Gevurah's constrictive condition.

Hod. The third gate and the eighth sephira. This feminine sephira is commonly called "Splendor." It is closely paired with Netzach, "Victory."

karma. In traditional Buddhist thinking, karma is a form of causality, an automatic consequence of existence itself, which is tied up both *within* this life and *between* present, past, and future lives. In this way, our actions have consequences both now and in future existences. We can also see circumstances that occur in this life as being the product of actions we made in previous existences. A kabbalistic understanding of this might be: karma is in effect a form of unconsciousness-in-action.

That is, we do something (good or bad) that has consequences in the future. According to the typical understanding of karma, what has been set in motion must be continued until the energy it holds is expended. The question arises: "What happens as a person gets more whole, more awake, and more connected to God? Must everything that is set in motion remain in motion?" The answer to that is yes and no. As we get more God-connected and surrender more to the Almighty, karma still exists and we are free of it at the same time. For instance, if you've ever tried to surf, you know that you must go with the force of the wave: when you lose the feel of the wave, its direction and velocity, you fall off. For an experienced surfer, the wave still exists but he or she is one with it, while a beginner is besieged by the wave. It is the same with karma: what we are besieged by in the universe of Assiyah we are more one with in Yetzirah. In Briah, this same karma becomes our way of serving God, and we thank the Unnamable for the opportunity (karma) that was presented to us and created by us at the same time, since it led to this moment of surrender.

kavannah. Devotion, intention, focus. While usually understood as a quality one can bring to a spiritual practice such as prayer, for example, kavannah can also be understood as a state of being in open presence. This allows us not only to bring this quality to specific practices, but also to see the world as the fulfillment of God's presence itself.

Keter. The tenth gate or first sephira. Expressed by the names "Crown" and "Nothingness," Keter is the sephira closest to the Ayn-Sof, and expresses most fully the will of the Almighty. It is considered one of the masculine Attributes.

klipot (klipah, sing.). Literally a "shell," "barrier," or "husk." In this case, the remnants of the original vessels of Light—the sephirot—which shattered during the first emanation. These fallen pieces of the good are seen as the source of evil in traditional Lurianic kabbalistic thinking. They can also be seen as essentially good—since they are of the same source as the sephirot—but separated from the source of goodness and therefore dissociated from the central purpose of our being. They can also be seen as protective, in that they do not allow the Light to enter a being until that being is integrated enough not to shatter in the Light's effulgence.

Malchut. The sephira farthest from Keter in the central column, it is the first gate or tenth sephira and considered feminine. Because it is closest to our world—and farthest from the ineffable Keter—this sephira is sometimes given the nickname "Evil," which does not connote any essential quality, but rather its distance from Keter. It is the dwelling place of the Shekinah, the Divine presence, and in some ways is the most easily accessible sephira for human beings to relate to.

Netzach. "Victory," "Eternal." The seventh sephira and the fourth gate.

nirvana. From the perspective of duality, Nirvana is everything duality is not: a place of unification; the state reached once we are not identified with the small-I; the cessation of birth and death. From the awakened perspective, however, nirvana and its opposite (samsara) are the same, and it is this realization that sets us free from thinking we are not already free. See also samsara.

samsara. Usually thought of as "this world," the world of birth, decay, and death. In this way samsara is the opposite of nirvana. It can also be seen, in its enlightened aspect, as the manifestation of the life of the spirit—in other words, the playing out of the enlightened life in the world of duality. Thus, it is not a "lower" place than nirvana, but the place where "form is form; emptiness, emptiness," the arena of our life in this world and our service to the God-spirit in all things. From this perspective, samsara is nirvana—and different at the same time. See also nirvana.

sephirot. The Tree of Life, or Etz Chaim, is composed of ten sephirot: Keter (Crown); Chochmah (Wisdom); Binah (Understanding); Hesed (Loving-kindness); Gevurah (Strength); Tiferet (Beauty); Netzach (Victory); Hod (Splendor); Yesod (Foundation); and Malchut (Sovereignty). One "non-sephira"—Da'at (Knowledge)—is sometimes pictured in the Etz Chaim. The traditional view is that the sephirot are the intermediaries between the Ayn-Sof and the contraction of the tzimtzum that we all find ourselves in. They allow us to bridge the unbridgeable gap between ourselves and God. The sephirot offer a ladder, so to speak, by which we can connect ourselves to this Light. From another point of view, the sephirot are more like Divine laws or utterances. They are the fundamental conditions that life in this universe finds itself in, and knowing how to cleave to these laws teaches us how to transform from separate-only beings to beings who are in relationship with the Almighty Spirit of life.

Shema. In the Jewish liturgy, the Shema is the supreme statement of faith in the Oneness of God. Composed of three passages taken from various portions of the Torah, the first invocation is usually translated as "Hear, (or Listen) O Israel, the Lord our God, the Lord is One." A nonliteral translation: "Listen, you who struggle with the meaning of Reality: Reality is One and not two." This translation has allowed me to see the vastness of this injunction and place my limited, separating view up against the supreme statement of the Oneness of God.

Tiferet. The sixth sephira and the fifth gate. Found in the central column of the Etz Chaim, it is usually translated as "Beauty." It is considered one of the masculine sephirot.

Torah. Traditionally, the Five Books of Moses (Genesis, Exodus, Leviticus, Numbers, and Deuteronomy); also known as the Pentateuch, the Old Testament, or the Hebrew Bible. The Torah is often included as five of the twenty-four books collectively known as the Tanach, which are the Five Books of Moses, the Prophets, and the Writings (Psalms, Proverbs, Job, The Song of Songs, Ecclesiastes, and so on). The foundational text of Judaism and the written law, the Torah is also the history of the Jewish people and the personages and events that have gone into making the Jewish people a nation. The written Torah and the Oral Torah—that portion of the Torah transmitted to and handed down by Moses and interpreted by generations of thinkers—combine to reveal what the Torah truly is: a description of the interaction between Oneness and duality; a vehicle for finding and cleaving to this Unity, often called God; and a profound explanation of the reasons and direction of Creation.

Tree of Life (Etz Chaim). There are several different versions of the Tree of Life, and two important kabbalistic books, the *Sefer ha-Yetzirah* and the *Sefer ha-Bahir,* mention early aspects of this schema, which reached its flowering in the work of Rabbi Isaac the Blind and, seminally, in that of Rabbi Isaac Luria, "the Ari." Embodying both the linear and holographic views of reality, the Tree of Life expresses the interrelationships between Divine Attributes, the pathways consciousness and energy follow in order to make up this world and everything in it, from the material universe to the inner psychological workings of the human mind and soul. In its inner teachings, it shows both the contradictions and synergy between Oneness and duality. The Tree of Life should not be looked at as simply a diagram or representation of Reality, but a doorway through which one can enter into communion with what is Real. It points the way to God.

tzaddik. "The righteous one"; a saintly teacher or person.

tzimtzum. In one of the most potent kabbalistic descriptions of the Creation process, the Divinity first withdraws its essence, to leave a vacated space where God is not, so that individual beings, no longer nullified in God's greater Light, can exist. This withdrawal or contraction is called the tzimtzum. While from the linear point of view the tzimtzum is an accurate picture of our exile from God, from the holographic point of view tzimtzum is a fiction, since the Shema teaches us that no place is devoid of the Divine. The understanding of the true nature of the tzimtzum, which calls for a reconciliation between Oneness and separateness, is part of the process by which we awaken into the presence of God.

yesod. The ninth sephira and the second gate. It is usually translated as "Foundation" and is associated with the genitals and the foundational concerns of procreation, connection, and relationship in our lives. It is considered a feminine sephira.

Yetzirah. The next most integrated universe after Assiyah. This world is the universe of *formation,* and it is transparent to—or contains—Assiyah. This is the universe of emotions and their angelic counterparts. The interiority of psychological thinking first makes its appearance here, and with that momentous occurrence, which shows the inner reasons for the actions we take in Assiyah, a new relationship with ourselves and the world arises. In Yetzirah—unlike in Assiyah, where the world and ourselves seem to be two separate things—we see that *we* are responsible for making the world as much as the world makes us. This brings us a new level of freedom and a new level of responsibility. See also Assiyah, Atzilut, Briah.